Blood on the Typewriter

The World of Philip White

ROBBIE BRECHIN

Wakefield Press

Wakefield Press
16 Rose Street
Mile End
South Australia 5031
www.wakefieldpress.com.au

First published 2021

Photograph gathering and retouching by Milton Wordley
Cover design by Liz Nicholson, Wakefield Press
Edited by Julia Beaven, Wakefield Press
Typeset by Michael Deves, Wakefield Press
Printed in Australia by Ovato Book Printing, formerly Griffin Press, Adelaide

ISBN 978 1 74305 812 1

NATIONAL LIBRARY OF AUSTRALIA

A catalogue record for this book is available from the National Library of Australia

CORIOLE
McLAREN VALE

Wakefield Press thanks Coriole Vineyards for continued support

Contents

Foreword
Brian Croser

There is and could only be one Philip. One is enough. I call him Philip, not 'Whitey' as the rest of the world does, not because of false decorum but out of fear. That fear is primal, born of my first encounter with him, sometime in the last millennium, probably the early 80s.

This wraith, a preacher's son, had appeared from over the hill, off the clack-stone plains and slopes of Kanmantoo, in a tasting room in the Adelaide CBD to conduct a tasting for *Winestate* magazine. I was a guest panellist, apparently feeling empowered enough to argue about some trivial aspect of the tasting protocol. I don't remember much about the tasting as the occasion was dominated by Philip's reaction to my impertinence. He grabbed a First World War bayonet used as a paperweight on his desk, and thumped it hilt-deep into the wooden tasting bench and growled, 'We'll do it my way!' We did it his way.

Like Wolf Blass I did my best to avoid Philip in social circumstances. Wolf was often a target of Philip's forensic insights and is believed to have grumbled in German, 'Can no one rid me of this turbulent priest?' – or something like that. Fortunately for Philip no one understood him. I walked on the other side of Rundle Street when passing the Exeter Hotel.

My fear of Philip was, on balance, outweighed by my admiration of his writing, while often disagreeing (not openly of course) with his opinions. Philip writes like a gun stockman uses a whip, with flourish, precision and a final crack. Pity the rump on the end of the lash flick. He also writes like a dreamy poet. Describing a wine from an admired vineyard and its winemaker's context, not for him the fruit and floral analogies, rather the full sensorial effect in words that make you want to taste it, in fact make you feel you are tasting it.

I could dwell on the many times he had issues with my public position: water into wine in the Riverland, the unnecessary extravagance of the National Wine Centre, my appropriation of the name Tapanappa, also the name of a formation within his beloved Kanmantoo geological group.

That's enough, suffice it to say Philip is the most gifted Australian wine writer, with added intellectual dimensions beyond wine, ranking in my mind with Hugh Johnson and Andrew Jefford in the sheer joy of using words like few others can.

Preface

Philip enters the outskirts of your life like a distant, faintly threatening figure in a long, hazy David Lean *Lawrence of Arabia* camera shot. When he finally arrives, you fear him a little more in close-up. Loud. Talks like an old man reading from a Quentin Tarantino script of unrelenting sadism. Unbidden, strangers gather, listening in awe, careful to dodge the spittle. Anger. Punishment. Darkness. Violence unimaginable. Word gets around. That's Philip C. White, the Kanmantoo Kid.

Should you get to know him, you will join a very large group. You'll love him for his discreet courage, cussed lack of interest in materialism, and the spooky way he can make you taste wine with his words. For his thoughtfulness. For his ability to make you feel better about yourself. For his bedazzling conversation. For his depth of knowledge on a big, fat range of topics and events. For his playful unpredictability. For his appearance of 'otherness'; someone with an extra layer of spinning atoms. Or you'll regard him as an argumentative, short-fused, auto-didactic know-it-all. Eyewitnesses say if Philip is in one of his moods, his festering glower can darken an entire conference hall.

An ex-lover, 'Nadine', put it this way: 'I didn't have the faintest idea where he was a lot of the time. I found that really difficult. He was very unreliable. But you learnt to live with it. If I want to have a relationship with the least boring person in Adelaide, this is what I have to put up with.'

Philip – many know him as 'Whitey' – has led a life that could be a film. Tension and drama aplenty. Romance. Adventure. Risk-taking. A man who cannot be held by speed limits. He has a beguiling way of sucking you into his orbit, be you Leonard Cohen, Paul Kelly, Tubby Justice, Lowell George of Little Feat. Maynard Keenan of Tool. Don Dunstan. David Gulpilil. Max Schubert. Peter Lehmann. He was trained as a child in the art of rock-hard, scary preaching of the Biblical message of destruction, anger, revenge and sadism. That dark art has been distilled into oratory so powerful that Philip can stand five steps back from a public bar counter and find himself encircled by a dozen entranced drinkers: cool-handed lawyers, bohemians, university students and council workers.

The most common description of his outward appearance is that he could be a bikie. Or, on a good day, a bikie in a suit and fedora, a stylish hat favoured by gangsters, businessmen and Johnny Depp . . . He can talk like a Murray Mallee farmer, squashing vowels like tin cans of West End beer. Many people of high calibre, especially in South Australia, eventually affect more modulated, posher tones. Not Philip. He's absolutely watertight sure of himself and his royal hickness.

Author and inventor Mark 'I tinker, therefore I am' Thomson remembers first sighting Philip at a party in the backyard of a house in Norwood in the late seventies, Eric Clapton's 'Layla' and the Allman Brothers on the soundtrack. 'He was standing there on his own, holding a glass of red wine. I thought, Ah, so that's Philip White. He wasn't yet being adored by his disciples – that was later in the evening.' As Mark and many others saw, the fledgling wine writer carried an air of practised raffishness. Of recklessness. Of you-think-you-know-me – but-you-never-will.

A man much mythologised. Willing to give the fables a helping hand. Up ahead, Philip faced up to heavy responsibilities. To Penfolds and its worldwide, seriously upmarket Grange. It is a gauge for the economic wellbeing of South Australia. An entrée to the swelling wealth of China. Call it our liquid Ferrari. He had to be fair and reasonable when analysing all wine – big and little. Along the way, Philip discovered a flair for composing wine bottle labels, among other things. But he himself cannot be labelled. Try to explain his ruthless, rebellious independence by raising the spectre of, say, Ernesto 'Che' Guevara and you will yell at your own folly. Nil resemblance. Yet you know you are trying to find shorthand for a bloke who has stood up for his beliefs, largely regardless of consequences. Enjoyed the odd junket to France and China – pure as driven snow.

The Kanmantoo Kid was a good shot who filled the family pot with rabbits when money for food was scarce. And when such exploits were kept hidden from neighbours, who derided the red-in-tooth-and-claw lack of sophistication, he flirted with poetry, music and painting, achieving varying degrees of success and acclaim.

But if he were just an incendiary wine writer, this story would begin and end fairly quickly. The key is the way a young man with a massive brain, an improbably sensitive nose for substances and chemicals and unlimited curiosity lived a life that is uncommon. It is arguably becoming more endangered, as the world becomes more competitive, materialistic and conservative.

There is some kind of life message in the fact that Philip is surrounded by friends who attend to his every wish and need as he copes with terminal cancer. In that, on a single, sun-cast morning, a couple of former lovers – together – pamper and feed him with grace and seamless ease. In that this gifted, cranky old bastard has more love within reach than most of us could ever hope for.

CHAPTER 1

The Kanmantoo Kid

'No, these people have guns. They don't like surprise visits. Can't go there.' – Philip, on a somewhat tense visit to his childhood town

'Kanmantoo' may be an Aboriginal word meaning 'different speech'. That claim, now popular online, cannot be authenticated, according to Professor Ghil'ad Zuckermann, Chair of Linguistics and Endangered Languages at the University of Adelaide. In any event, it is the French who have the nutshell way of describing the dusty edge-of-the-Mallee town a 25-kilometre drive from Mt Barker: *jolie laide*, 'ugly pretty'. It can be attractively leafy and idyllic. Or it can be raggedly, mood-lowering rocky. A miles-from-nowhere mining community that was home to a sensitive young man with a foghorn voice and an attitude.

When Philip recalls the big family shift from Victoria, made in 1959 when he was aged seven, he provides a clue to his unusually close relationship to the country.

> I grew up on the snow on mountain ash forests in the Central Highlands. It was beautiful. Cool summers. And to arrive in Kanmantoo in the spring, when everything was rocky, no cattle. There were sheep, which were filthy to us; they stank. Everything was wrong. In the summer, everything died away.

The miners of the 1800s cleared all the trees and scrub around Callington and Kanmantoo to fire the copper smelters. The land was 'bare and troubled'. And the weather could be scary. 'Thunderstorms in the hills to the north would dump an inch of rain in just an hour or so,' Philip wrote in his blog, drinkster.com:

> As there was no vegetation to hold it, that water would simply skim off the hillsides to flash-flood our house and wash cars off the main street into the Big Erosion that joined the Bremer four miles downstream at Callington. People died.

While Philip has been known to complain about the isolation and the very hot, windy, dusty summers, his upbringing was typical of rural South Australia in the sixties. Lots of leeway for all-day adventure with his siblings. Swimming in a dam on the nearby Bremer River. Cowboys and Indians. Later, not just toy guns – real rifles. Philip dips into memory: 'We'd go swimming in the river at Murray Bridge after the hellish heatwave bus ride home from school at Mount Barker,' he writes in drinkster.com:

> C'mon youse: Mum, six kids, in the car, seventeen miles, straight in the river. We'd slop around in there for hours, swimming over to the other bank and upstream around the bridge pylons. You could catch the odd Murray cod and freshwater cray and even see underwater until the cheese factory pumped so much junk into the river you could only catch redfin on cheddar. No one ever swallowed.

It is a warm summer's day in 2019. The tall, rangy man who was that child is in the passenger seat of a car in the Adelaide Hills. A savage year has crept up on him, and he is, with every slight tremor and overly cautious step, a man approaching seventy at a faster pace than he arrived at the turn of sixty. A wicked intruder has scrubbed out the youthful patina of only a couple of years before. We are on the road, the better to explore his crucible, Kanmantoo.

Philip is in his pyjama bottoms and slippers. A mighty, fluffy Russian officer's fur hat adds to the air of eccentricity. Fair enough to say he looks like an escapee from *One Flew Over The Cuckoo's Nest*. On this day, doctors don't know if their intensive treatment is killing the cancer or their patient. Each day brings different nuances. The patient is just that, bearing with surprisingly good grace the slings and arrows of nuclear medicine and the way it stomps all over him like a back alley thug.

We pull up by the Kanmantoo copper mine that once provided work for him, Pastor Jimmy, and his brothers. Philip has learned much about the earth and its dirty secrets. He never qualified as a geologist, but he can talk about soils and rocks as if he had put them in the ground himself. We take photographs. Not ten minutes have elapsed before a white ute turns the corner to our right, slowly passing, driver waving. 'They're checking on us,' Philip says. 'That's mine security.'

The journey takes on a little more tension. It's not a joyride. Philip is dangerously ill, and we are neither strangers nor buddies. Childhood landmarks come and go by. The house where two lesbians ruled the roost like landed gentry. The home of a bloke who probably shot Aboriginals many years ago. Up a side road, Philip points to a vineyard he planted as a teenager. His broad shoulders are testament – he wasn't scared of hard labour. As the car progresses, the agitation in Philip rises. He says nothing until he is virtually level with the vines.

'We can't go any further,' he says, tone-of-voice backing up his mild panic.

'Why not?'

'Because we haven't said we're coming.'

'So? We're not arriving anywhere.'

'No, these people have guns. They don't like surprise visits.'

It isn't until much later, when Philip talks about living in Cape Fear, that the penny drops. It happens to be the title of a 1962 psychological thriller starring Robert Mitchum, one of Philip's favourite actors. *Variety* described Mitchum's performance as a 'menacing omnipresence'. Add 'steady and starkly sinister style' from another source.

He says:

> See, every night after dinner, or tea as we called it, there'd be a reading from the Old Testament, a reading from the New Testament. And then a long story from the history of Protestantism. It'd be like the Dominicans slaughtering the villagers in Switzerland and putting live cats in their wounds. Horrific. So we'd go to bed every night with that in our heads. The imagery we grew up with was probably worse than what kids see now on television.

The man running that show was Pastor Jimmy White. Philip's father. Eldest son:

> If he walked in here now he would have a good gentleman's Akubra with a suit and tie and he always had really good shoes.
>
> He would be very formal. He would unsettle everyone in the room, without saying anything. And attract their attention, without knowing what he was going to say himself. He would change the atmosphere without even knowing what he was going to say, without even saying anything, or knowing who was in the room. You see that with actors, like Mitchum.

Mitchum is again mentioned for his role in *Ryan's Daughter*, a film in which he reminded Philip of his father. Next in that line-up is Burt Lancaster in *Elmer Gantry* and Robert Duvall in *The Apostle*, portraying a charismatic preacher 'of a good order'. Without giving anything away, 'charisma' is the word Philip uses to describe the positive side of his father, Pastor Jimmy. That speaks not of paternal warmth, of Jimmy casting an arm around his son's shoulder and talking about the bouncy-castle happenstance of a big world outside. That form of ease was never on the cards for any of the brood.

> My father was a really charismatic man. A storyteller. I equate that mysterious, admirable side of him with his attractiveness to women, because women really liked him. They found him pretty horny. He had a film-star quality.

Anyone looking for Jimmy, as it were, can glean clues as Philip recalls being taken under the wing of a nurse, who was older and more worldly.

> I met her through my father's preaching in Renmark. It had to be a secret, but she took me to the cinema to see *Ryan's Daughter*. As soon as Robert Mitchum came on in his woollen singlet I could smell my father. She later told me I squeezed her hand too hard at that point. That woman taught me a lot that was good, without fucking. [Chuckles.] She never crossed the River Styx. I was still in high school. She was the first woman who advised me my father was sexy.
>
> And she said I was like him.

CHAPTER 2

Poppa Sizz and the Scarlet Whore

'The King James Bible was the biggest influence on my writing.'
– Philip White

Philip has supped literary influence from many different cups. But more than a few have detected the Bible as the cornerstone of his style, both verbally and in print. 'The visions are astonishing. If you know the Book of Revelations inside out, man, you don't need to go to the movies. *Armageddon*, *Dark Rider*, the Scarlet Whore . . .'

The good Lord was omnipresent at home. Mum Sylvia's own father, Ted, had been a street preacher in Melbourne. Philip knew Ted as Poppa Sizz, a man who spent much of his time broadcasting hot gospel from his blood-red removal van, the 'Red Terror'. It was painted with Bible texts aimed at the lost souls on the streets of Melbourne.

Poppa showed the very young Philip his place of work, and its Tower of Power: a huge vat of white-hot, boiling liquid salt. To him, the vat was a reminder of the fires of Hell. Philip: 'Little Philip never forgot that. It was a threat. I've never liked being threatened.'

Not far away in Melbourne was a youthful Jimmy White, desperately searching for a path to worshipping a god that suited his particular beliefs. Poppa Sizz gave Jimmy the chance to preach on his rip-it-up frontline, outside a Richmond pub at closing time, preaching massacre and assorted horrific punishments for sinners. But it wasn't all vengeance and sadism and fearfully following commandments from on high. Sylvia, one of Poppa's beautiful daughters, caught Jimmy's eye.

His preaching efforts so impressed his God-fearing sweetheart that she spent her entire life supporting and encouraging him in his relentless service of their Lord. She'd had one chance to flee social suffocation and mount what would have been an almost unthinkable act of defiance against her father. At the sweet age of sixteen, she made a run for it to Sydney with big sister Kath. It all fell apart when Poppa Sizz found Kath's Bible in a second-hand bookshop. And tracked them both down.

> Poppa Sizz set in train a chain of fierce evangelical faith that has extended for four generations. It was a life without the luxury we measure in physical goods, but one built tightly around the non-conformist Protestant Christian family. We lived according to 2 Corinthians 6:17: 'Come out from among them, and be ye separate, saith the Lord, and touch not the unclean [thing].'

Philip's paternal grandfather, Poppa, was a WWI veteran.

> Poppa had shell shock, which nobody else understood. I understood it, as his first grandson. I knew Pop was really sick. He had two sons, Robert and my father Jimmy. Uncle Robert was an alcoholic and a violent man. Poppa would shake his head and say, 'I don't know what I've done. I've got two sons and one of them is a madman through religion and the other one's a madman for the booze.'

CHAPTER 3

Manic Street Preachers

'Philip would have to stand there and preach and all his schoolmates would be hooning past and yelling: "Ah, Philip, ya bloody clown."'

– Mark Thomson, founder and research director of the Institute of Backyard Studies, author of several books and fellow 'know-it-all'

While gambling doesn't appear to loom large in the White family backdrop, the move from Victoria to South Australia was a seat-of-the-pants expedition in 1959.

> Dad was invited by a group of dissolute non-conformists in South Australia who needed a preacher. So he gave his farm to his brother, shed himself of all his worldly goods and took a small amount of money and a new car and brought us four kids to SA.

Philip looks back with some fondness – the outdoors suited him and his boisterous siblings. Rock music and TV were outlawed, but guns were encouraged. 'You know we used to hang a net over an old mine shaft and hang a brother down a rope and get fifty pigeons and just pluck them and put them in the pot,' Philip tells me. 'We all ate really well considering there was no money. Dad wasn't very good at shooting but, luckily, Uncle Donald was a champion outdoor sportsman. He was a dry fly fisherman and he taught me a lot about hunting.'

His Dad's congregation used to donate all sorts of sustenance.

> You know, there'd always be someone bringing half a sheep or a gallon of milk. People would bring us furniture and clothes; we were the clearing house for a lot of missionaries around the world. People used to bring us all their old clothes and we'd sort them and send them to different places. We'd pick the eyes out of all those clothes donated for the missionaries [big, long cackle]. That's where we got all our clothes.

As the White boys grew, so did their armoury. Philip is already chuckling, and he's only just begun his yarn about the casual growth of the gun collection.

> I'll never forget one day we had a white missionary come over from the Congo. Africa was on fire and here was this poor bloke looking through our bedroom window – he'd just come from the slaughter in the Congo. He asked my mum: 'Why have they got so many guns?' And my mum said: 'If we don't let them have guns, they'll be going to the Strathalbyn dances.' And that was considered the perfect answer [loud cackle-laugh]. Oh yeah, we had rapid-fire guns. Before John Howard you could get automatics. I can't remember ever registering a gun.

Journalist Terry Plane recalls taking a drive to Murray Bridge late one night.

> As I came into Kanmantoo, I heard what sounded like rifle fire and I saw a bunch of blokes standing by the side of the road and I thought: Gunshot. Kanmantoo. Has to be the White boys. Sure enough it was. We stayed and had a few more drinks. Went to a dam in the Bremer River. Philip, Paul, Stephen and Andrew were there. They all stripped naked and jumped in the water. For some reason, I had a dress of my mother's in the boot of my car. I was meant to take it to the dry cleaners. So I put that on and joined them. [Laughs] This was around dawn, in summer.

Stephen White, two years younger than Philip and with a successful career in mining behind him, recalls:

> Up until a certain age, there was only one gun, and that was Dad's .22. He didn't hunt but he used to shoot the birds out in the yard or galahs in our orchard. I reckon [younger brother] Paul might have been fifteen when he bought his first .22. You didn't need a licence. I bought two guns from the bloke down the Kanmantoo shop, but he didn't sell them there. Say I wanted a 30-30 lever-action Winchester – he'd go to the warehouse in Adelaide and buy it and he'd take his little bit for selling to me.

Stephen is less forthcoming about the exact power of the White collection. 'Machine guns? Aw, Paul had a lot of weird things.' Philip added: 'Uncle Philip had a zip action .22 that could shoot a whole magazine with one pull of the trigger. About ten bullets. I remember him hitting a possum and it looked like it had just been unzipped, up the middle.'

Philip's first serious girlfriend, 'exotic Estonian' and older woman Maire Mannik, recalls a car ride with Philip, who was an unknown quantity at the time. 'It was full of Bibles,' she noted. 'It was his father's car; his own would have had a gun or two.' Philip and his siblings spent more than the average amount of time hunting – shooting, fishing and trapping. The absence of TV and radio in the White household wasn't a matter of economics but religious beliefs. Philip:

> I was allowed to have records, because I think Mum and Dad thought I needed some entertainment. But I wasn't allowed to have Devil's music, so nothing with an African beat. I couldn't play Gun, a British guitar trio who had a hit with 'Race With The Devil', or the Stones' 'Little Red Rooster'. But I did have Johnny Cash and when I played my old man Johnny Cash and June

Carter in *The Holy Land* he was amazed. Dad loved the Band's *Music From Big Pink*; I could get away with Joan Baez, and then the acoustic – though not electric – Bob Dylan.

The absence of TV in Kanmantoo carried over into the rest of Philip's adult life. It could be argued that it had a considerable impact on the way he thought, how his imagination flexed. It takes a strong will to mix socially and not have anything to contribute to conversations on *The Man From Uncle*, *Homicide*, *The Box*, *Steptoe and Sons*, *Seinfeld* or *Game of Thrones*. The late author Roald Dahl, a favourite with young readers, saw TV as 'a monster, a nauseating, unclean fool'.

It is not easy to find conclusive evidence that what is these days laughably called the 'small screen' is detrimental to daydreaming. So, it may be pure coincidence that a country boy stimulated by outdoor adventure and comics like *The Eagle* and *The Beano* grew up to be a writer, one regarded by some as one of the best and certainly most distinctive writers of his chosen genre – wine – in the world.

Signs of promise were always hovering. Runner-up for the Tennyson Medal for English. Glowing reports from an English teacher. One of the most alluring pieces of evidence takes shape in correspondence, when Whitey-in-his-twenties was recommended as a pen pal to a seventeen-year-old woman in Brisbane. Herewith is a portion of Whitey's response to the first missive from Tubby Justice, later an acclaimed singer-songwriter in Adelaide in the eighties and nineties.

'*You hunt me in my most comfortable places*,' he writes in his impeccable, small longhand,

> *. . . you make me your toy.*
> *It is not simple, this feeling for which you ask.*

> *Do you demand warmth? Is it the paper, or the time?*
> *Why do you hide yourself?*

Then: '*You have addressed an apprentice man, prone to throw-away wondering. I am thin, I have little to offer.*'

The White clan loved trips back to Victoria for visits to Mum's parents in Melbourne or Dad's folks in the Gippsland. All up, there were six children so preparation was paramount. Food and drink had to be prepared and packed for fast-growing lads cooped up on a long, radio-free journey.

> Mum grew up in Richmond, in the slums of Burnley. All her sisters seemed to work in the rag trade. So they all had contacts, they were dressmakers and sewers and stuff. Mum knew where to get the best clothes at a discount. So she would take us to Dimmey's department store and buy us really good clothes.

A pure kind of sensuous joy fills his face as he reveals: 'I had the best shoes at school.' The easiest book to find at home was the Bible. According to the Old Testament, which Philip and his siblings knew by heart, God was:

> A control freak. Vindictive. Misogynistic. Homophobic. Sado-masochistic. Genocidal. Racist. Was volcanically, monstrously angry much of the time. If you weren't with him, you'd be slaughtered. Your wives would be ravished and your 'infants dashed to pieces' on rocks.

Earlier in his pastoral career, Jimmy had flirted with the Methodists. When working as a Methodist lay preacher in South East Gippsland in Victoria, Jimmy abruptly quit because, as Philip put it, 'They were going to have a dance in the hall.'

What came next was a brutal swerve to the religious right – the Exclusive Brethren. 'We became Brethren, exclusive, very conservative,' Philip says. 'There was a while when we weren't allowed to have clothes with zips or anything too flashy. I couldn't believe the darkness of that religion. It was all little meetings in houses rather than in the church. Very dark and repressive.' It was forbidden for anyone to go to university – and thus be infected by modern ideas or the theory of evolution. That is explained by another directive: that members keep themselves separate from other people as far as possible because of the belief that the world is a place of wickedness.

While Pastor Jimmy eventually cut ties with the Brethren because he didn't agree with a rule that they could take your children away in certain circumstances, he kept many of their beliefs – and that made primary school difficult for Philip.

> It was horrid. Because if you're sitting in a classroom and you've been told that the teacher is a sinner and you think you're the only one in the school who's going to go to heaven if Jesus comes back, it's not very good for your social life.
>
> In a sense, it put a lot of street sass into me. I learnt about survival in a similar way to a junkie's kid. That sense of being different and not being part of a gang. I put all my effort into creativity and being a skite in a sense, pleasing teachers with dazzling essays and poems, which gave me a bit of confidence that I could write. That carried me over.
>
> At high school I was quite popular among the students. I was elected head prefect. The headmaster, when he found out I'd won the vote, came in and re-counted. So I immediately became deputy head prefect. [Laughs/coughs]

As he approached the leaving-home age, Philip became bolder in defiance of the ultra-strict Jimmy. Yearning for the adolescent thrill of peeking over the hills that separated Kanmantoo from the city, Philip would sneak away.

> I'd take sickies from school – it was matriculation year. Mum and Dad didn't know where I was. So I started hitchhiking. One day I ran into some doctors' daughters from Wattle Park. They had an underground poetry magazine called *Dark Areas* [more chuckling].

It was wind-in-the-hair time when Philip found even more reliable freedom, in a shed in Pinnaroo. A 1947 Chrysler DeSoto, all thick, swollen metal. A sexy monster in the hulking American way.

> A bloke had got it for his wedding. But he then bought a truck and never used that car again. Hadn't been driven in thirty years. I paid fifteen pounds. We put a new battery in it, put some new tyres on it, put some petrol in it and started her up.

What would be regarded as a swaying death trap today enabled Philip to travel far and wide, at something approaching the velocity he craved. The DeSoto had a soft, floating ride and a recirculating ball steering system so loose it would scare modern drivers. A 3.9-litre side valve flat head straight six. During one set of school holidays, Philip left the car at home while he was away working for extra pocket money at a mine in Cobar in central New South Wales. The DeSoto was gone when he returned. What happened?

> The old man sold it to a bloke who later made a dune buggy out of it, for forty-five pounds, thirty pounds more than I'd paid for it. Dad did that behind my back so I couldn't drive away anymore. That was him showing me that I shouldn't go anywhere.
>
> These were the Brethren family values. Stay at home and keep to yourselves. (Strangely prophetic, given coronavirus.)

Good friend and likeable eccentric Mark Thomson:

One of my most distinctive memories of Philip is finding out about his religious background. Wow, fascinating. This whole network of fundamentalists out in the bush. Those conservative religious organisations are still travelling the back roads. In Philip's childhood, he was obliged by his father to be a preacher in the main street of Murray Bridge. I remember Philip telling me about how he and his four brothers would stand there, Bibles in hand preaching, their father in the background. Philip would have to stand there and preach and all his schoolmates would be hooning past and yelling, 'Ah, Philip, ya bloody clown.'

Everybody's yelling at him. He once gave a demo in the front bar of the Exeter of what he had to do. It was amazing, watching those at the front bar retreat to the other end by the pool table because there was a lot of spit. There was me, grinning like a goon, standing next to Philip doing the full fire-and-brimstone number. Everyone else is clustered down by the pool table saying, 'Philip's gone off again.' The stories he told me revealed a whole underworld of rural religious preaching stuff.

You wonder, just how did that inform the rest of his life?

CHAPTER 4

Four Fat Coppers

'They strip-searched me. I had mushrooms in my jocks.' – Philip

If one Philip interlude explains him more fully than any other, it is the one about the Four Fat Coppers in the Adelaide Hills in 1974. It's the equivalent of an Enid Blyton series for adults, with Philip's Mallee speech pattern on high. Paul Hogan, former Sydney Harbour Bridge rigger, was on the rise as a TV comedian, and the unconventional Sgt Donger might well have appeared in a comedy sketch based on Philip's stimulant-hunting confrontation with the officers.

The incident was reported much later, one July day in 2018, when Philip was deep in conversation about his life for the purposes of this book. He was not then aware that much of his imposing 184-centimetre frame was heaving with cancer. Up his spine, making a move for his brain. Melting his groin. Teeming in his torso. Sick as he was (though not knowing what precisely was wrong) he dragged into sequence every atom he could, in a bravura performance. On display was the man who had turned heads all over the world, over five decades. The transcript of the four-hour session was mesmerising. It began with Philip's plan to take the Overland train to Canberra, to visit one of his four brothers, second-eldest Stephen. He was accompanied by his first serious girlfriend, Maire Mannik. As with his first three lovers, she was older – twenty-six to his twenty.

> I thought I'd take some magic mushrooms with me. To give me and my brother a sandwich. So I'm in this paddock at the back of the Stirling railway station, which was infamous for gold tops. And I'd got a 10-gallon hat full of 'em in about twenty minutes. And when I got back through the gate, in the hedgerow, there were four big fat coppers. Two on either side, jumped on me:
>
> 'Gotcha!'
>
> 'What are you going to do with those toadstools?'
>
> 'You can eat 'em.'
>
> 'Why are you going to eat them?'
>
> 'Bit like getting drunk, slightly intoxicating.'
>
> 'You're getting LSD, aren't ya?'
>
> 'No, no, LSD doesn't grow in a paddock.'
>
> 'How do you know that?'

Philip continues:

> They strip-searched me. I had mushrooms in my jocks. They wouldn't believe I was picking those toadstools, thought I was an idiot telling lies. Searched my car. The boot was full of lucerne hay me and my girlfriend used for the guinea pigs. It was all loose leaf and they thought, Look at this! They thought it was marijuana.
>
> They kept me for about two hours and were about to let me go without charge. Nothing to charge me with. One of them said, 'We'd better ring the Drug Squad.' There was a thing called the *Psychotropic and Narcotics Drugs Act*. In those days, there were a lot of scares about people smoking banana skins and shooting up Vegemite. So they had this law whereby without an Act of Parliament, all it took was the Police Commissioner, the Health

Minister and a doctor – something like that – to add a substance to that list. It would be gazetted in the Gazette, but there was no change to the actual law, they could just add things ad hoc.

I could hear the Drug Squad bloke: 'What, you've got mushrooms? Hang on, they're illegal now.'

So I was charged. It was a test case. And the lawyers all thought the mushrooms would be somewhere between acid and heroin and I'd go to jail. It kept getting listed in higher courts. Every time I went to court they told me to bring a book and a toothbrush. It was really quite frightening. I was in and out of court for nearly a year, I reckon. Eventually, I got an enormous fine and a suspended sentence. The fine was about a third of my annual income.

Eventually, I got to Canberra. My brother Stephen was a garbage collector to Governor-General Sir John Kerr. So somewhere in this house here, I've got a box with John Kerr's toothbrush and aftershave.

Maire Mannik remembers Philip was unemployed at the time, and she says the mushrooms were collected from under the pine trees at Marbury School in Aldgate, not near the railway station. 'Yes he had a hat full of them. The cops thought it was a marijuana plantation. Psilocybin had been made illegal the day before. Bad luck. It was heard in the Magistrates Court and took all of five minutes. Guilty plea and a $100 fine. I paid for the entire thing.'

CHAPTER 5

Mining Philip's Mind

'It is a pity there are not more people like him.'
– Robert James Champion de Crespigny, AC

When you hear that wealthy businessman Robert James Champion de Crespigny, AC, twice in a row won the *Vogue* magazine award for being South Australia's best-dressed man, you wonder how much he has in common with Philip. And you keep on raising an eyebrow when the former Melbourne Grammar student and SA Great South Australian of the Year adds: 'I cannot personally recall ever being in the Exeter Hotel.' Yet, despite having – to this day – never set foot in his hired consultant's hallowed office/temple/theatre, de Crespigny was welcomed into Philip's domain, albeit always at another hotel, usually in North Adelaide.

We are assured the two men found much in common, even though de Crespigny tends to speak in the cautious, flat tones of a hard-nosed businessman. It's not until his voice becomes more musical, more relaxed, that you can start believing the 'company line'. And it helps to hear him finish his yarn on being *Vogue*'s best-dressed South Australian male with a playful confession: 'I got sacked in the third year because the person who'd nominated me had only seen photos of me in the paper, when I always wore a suit. What she didn't realise is I'm far more used to wearing short pants and a collared T-shirt. So I got expelled from that position.'

Philip White appeared in de Crespigny's orbit thanks to Caroline McFarlane, who, under the surname of Ainslie, appeared in hundreds of thousands of Adelaide homes every night reading the Channel 9 news. She later helped run a business offering media training, among other skills. Meanwhile, de Crespigny was a budding mining magnate with Normandy, on the hunt for someone who could lead him and his senior executives through the rocky hazards of TV, radio and newspapers.

Caroline does not agree Philip and the miner were, on paper, ill-suited as personalities. 'They are not an unlikely partnership,' she says.

> They are very comparable. It's not always obvious, but don't you think if you look at those two men, both are very successful at what they choose to do and they're totally disinterested in the superficial markers of accent or clothing? Highly intelligent. A lot of enthusiasm. Both of them have minds that can solve problems. Philip might rage at the world but then he'll stop, and say, 'This is the way we fix it.

Robert de Crespigny has no doubts:

> As soon as I met Philip, I warmed to him. Although he always looked somewhat dishevelled, and probably did not own any formal or 'neat' clothes, his character, smile and easy-to-engage nature always meant he was fun and delightful to be with. We discussed politics, wine, business, Indigenous affairs and life. People like him expand one's knowledge and are just fun to be around.
>
> Although I loved it, life as a CEO/chairman can be somewhat isolated and he certainly helped alleviate that as he was such

> a relaxing person to be with. I have always wanted to build relationships with people from different walks of life, as I feel that is so much better than always mixing with like-minded people.

de Crespigny, who was clearly no-nonsense about the actual business of running a company, nonetheless said:

> I think the biggest similarity is that I hope people would say we don't take ourselves seriously. I don't think he takes himself seriously. I'm talking just day-to-day life and mucking around with people. Life should be enjoyed. Be relaxed and comfortable about it and accept other people's arguments.

Philip is his usual cut-through self when he describes his former client as a 'droll accountant', who carefully watched the mining world and worked out that he might be able to do better than some of the 'idiots' already in it. In the end, Normandy was a world-class gold producer and de Crespigny walked away in 2002 with what some estimate to be adjacent to AU$100 million, a figure not confirmed by the boss. 'I really enjoyed working with him,' Philip says, beaming.

> He took my advice. No good being a consultant to anybody who doesn't do what you tell them to do. We were quite trusting and intimate. We talked over each other, but we each heard exactly what the other was saying. He paid me very well.

Robert de Crespigny was domiciled in England for many years but has returned to live in Adelaide and keeps in touch with his unlikely soothsayer. Philip recalls: 'Robert's secretary, Mary, would ring me on a Friday, probably about 5 to 5.30 pm.'

> Mary: 'Are you wearing a suit?'
> 'Well, no.'

Mary: 'You're in the Exeter, aren't you?'
'Yes.'
Mary: 'Pop home and put a suit on and Robert will pick you up in twenty minutes.'

'I have never heard about Philip being asked if he was in a suit,' de Crespigny says: 'That is not something I would ever ask but maybe my secretary did, unbeknownst to me. We certainly went off and had a drink together at various places where we hopefully would not be interrupted, like he would have been at the Exeter.'

de Crespigny is unwavering in his admiration for Philip:

> He was always a happy-go-lucky character. The Philip I knew, and I am sure he has not changed, was 'his own man'. He was true to himself, to what he believed and to his friends. In this current age, you are perhaps not allowed to say that 'he was a man'.
>
> The people who admire Philip admire him because he is what he is; what you see is what you get. It is a pity there are not more people like him.

Caroline McFarlane says she knew early on that Philip would be a good fit with the environmentally aware miner side of de Crespigny. 'Philip was the very first person who talked to me, in the late eighties, about fragile rivers, that rivers weren't just there to plunder.'

'South Australians won't fight for their water rights,' McFarlane – a water activist now living in Sydney – says.

> The Wentworth Group of concerned scientists, economists and business people wanted to halt everything on the Murray–Darling basin and do an audit of the money and the water. That hasn't happened at all. The only people who have fought for the river have been [former No Pokies Senator] Nick Xenophon and

> [former SA Premier] Jay Weatherill. When Philip reviews wine, he's never schizophrenic. He was so against excessive irrigation. He knew then it was destructive. So he didn't just stand there and say something else, he stood up with his words and fought for the river. You know exactly what his principles are. And he will fight for those who can't fight. I've seen him.

McFarlane tells a story that reveals a lot about Philip. It points to his mischievous streak, allied to his (autodidactic) desire to teach others what he has himself learned outside of academia.

> My twin boys, Angus and James, were at primary school. They came in to the 9 newsroom all down in the dumps. They didn't win Show and Tell.
>
> I went into the whole mother thing, 'oh no, it's best just to participate, don't worry it's not about winning'. Philip turned round and said, 'Oh shut up. It's all about winning'. Two days later, Philip had two boxes with lids bearing the seal of the South Australian Museum. Took off the top, and there were two animal skulls.
>
> Philip said they had belonged to a koala and a monkey. Anyway, the boys took them to the next Show and Tell and came rushing in to tell us how well they'd gone. The boys are now adults and they work all over the world, but in our house are these boxes with skulls saved from the dump when Philip took them from museum staff worried about having no space left.
>
> They formed their own relationship with this extraordinary, glorious mind. James is an engineer, worked in China, Indonesia and Brunei. Angus is a water scientist. But Philip was this wonderful person to them. His mind is . . . it's glorious and big and he embraces you, there's nothing frightening about him. It's a glorious encompassing mind in a glorious energetic body. Philip, as a wine blogger, I remember a line of his: 'We export water to China.' Meaning our precious water, via wine. He was fearless

in saying, yes, agriculture is important, wine is important – but don't trash it. I hadn't been worried about water at all. It was only when I was approached by Philip that I thought, Bloody hell, the foxes are in charge of the hen house here. You know what he does to your mind, he makes things go 'thwock' and you think differently about things. He calls me 'comrade'.

CHAPTER 6

Odd Couple

'I'd rather be a famous poet than a successful jeweller'
– Albert Bensimon, friend and benefactor

Odd couples pepper history and Philip has several of his own versions of the close relationship between neat freak Felix Ungar and fun-loving, casually clad bachelor Oscar Madison. The mild-mannered, immaculately dressed Albert Bensimon and Philip, the freewheeler who preferred the 'unmade bed' look, first met in the Exeter Hotel on Rundle Street. The sometimes loud-mouthed Philip was much more in tune with the pub itself, which resembled an abandoned building due to owner Nick Binns' instinct that it wasn't suited to the brassy, upmarket look of other pubs. The Exeter has stubbornly clung to the peeling paint era, and prospered. As in all fictionally based relationships, however, there was one sharp character reversal in this odd couple. Philip was the fine wine connoisseur and Bensimon his student.

> I met Philip in the mid-eighties. I walked into the Exeter pub on Rundle Street and ordered wine, because the wine list was particularly good. They told me it was Philip who did their list. Somebody pointed him out to me in the bar, and I introduced myself and the friendship grew from there.
>
> Philip used to hold court; it was his pub. He wouldn't sit at the bar, he'd stand back and people would gather around him.

The Exeter was famous for many things, among which was the best-priced Krug in the whole of Adelaide. You could buy a bottle there for almost the wholesale price – $140 as opposed to $200. It was a very unlikely place, full of students who couldn't afford Krug anyway. Philip picked good wines, for a pub budget. But there was never a bad wine.

There were lots of characters there. I remember one, Laurent, from Belgium. I asked him, in French, what he did for a living. He replied: *Je suis un tailleur de fleurs*, which translates to 'I am a tailor of flowers'. He was a gardener for the Port Adelaide Council. We always bought him drinks. A nice guy, probably an alcoholic. He got fined in the middle of one night for urinating in the street and had to organise to pay the fine at five dollars a month. Then, he got a letter from Belgium. Some relative had died and left him $17,000. So he took his first-ever flight to go home to collect the cash. Philip gave a fabulous eulogy at Laurent's funeral, and may still have his ashes, I'm not sure. It was the first and only funeral I'd ever been to where everybody in the room actually wanted to be there. Because, you go to funerals out of obligation or respect. A cousin dies, a neighbour dies, even if you don't like them, you go. But no one in that room had been employed by Laurent or been his employer. It was only people who had been fond of Laurent. I've seen 500 people at a funeral, but they're not 500 people who were close to the deceased.

I was thinking the other day, when it looked like Philip was on his last legs, I thought the best person to write his eulogy would be Philip. He writes so beautifully. And he knows himself very well, which is not always the case. He is very self-aware. Now, we're not quite sure what the prognosis is, but whenever the time comes, Philip should do his own eulogy.

Bensimon, who is a believer in philanthropy, is happy to admit to wishing he could walk at least a mile in Philip's boots of

Spanish leather, maybe with a bit of that distinctive swagger-cum-sway. He recalls a long-ago job interview question:

> Would I rather be a famous poet or the owner of a high-rise apartment block? I put down high-rise apartment block. But really, I'd rather be a famous poet. I later talked to the boss and he said: 'Yes, we knew you lied. We thought, if you're prepared to lie to answers to get the job, you might be prepared to embellish the product you're going to be selling on our behalf.'

Albert laughs, adding:

> Ain't that interesting? I'd much rather die and leave a half-a-dozen poems or a book behind that somebody would be reading in fifty years' time than a jewellery shop that won't exist. Wouldn't it be nice to be Philip White and leave something behind that people will read.
>
> Because money comes and money goes, you know. Philip had a choice. He could have sold his soul and made a lot of money. He could have started a website selling wines, why didn't he promote a wine and sell it? A lot of people gave him advice along those lines but he won't do it. I told him that with his drinkster.com blog, he could sell advertising space. He said he would never do that. He won't because readers might think he only liked a wine because the makers advertised it on his blog, or something like that; they may not think he's 100 per cent genuine.

CHAPTER 7

Hello Darkness, My Old Friend

'He has always been like a six-foot VU meter in relation to bullshit.' – Gus Howard

Filmmaker Gus Howard (*Blue Heelers, Backs to the Blast*) and Philip have known one another for more than four decades. Their relationship is built not only on a shared love of playing music and making films but also on a set of beliefs that no one ever wrote down, mainly because the bonds are intangible. Ideas, dreams and instincts, as well as the impact of refreshed social protocols and experimental tastes of the era. 'Put it this way,' Gus says,

> if I got arrested in Tangier and got to make only one phone call, it'd be to Philip. I wouldn't want him to get on a plane. He'd do it all right there, from where he was. And I'd do the same. Apart from my family – my wife and my son – my relationship with Philip is probably the next most important in my life. We've never had an argument, though he has fallen out with a lot of people and pissed them off.

The high level of mutual trust is deepened by Philip's sensitivity to the invisible atoms flying around him, explained in terms of a device measuring the signal level in audio equipment. 'He has always been like a six-foot VU meter in relation to bullshit and the truth,' Gus says. 'Needle swinging all over the place, often in the red. You could trust it, too. His reactions to situations would result in something said that left nothing to add. This is why people confide in him.'

Almost without exception, friends and acquaintances, lovers and enemies talk about Philip's relationship with the truth. When admirers speak of his unwavering authenticity, they highlight his wilful refusal to compromise beliefs for mere financial gain. The truth of the matter is always paramount. And to give credit where it is due, we must thank Pastor Jimmy White.

The narcissistic, sadistic father who never gave his eldest son an inch – except when it came to beating him in a coolly expert way with the three-foot cable of an electric kettle.

'It's just possible one of the things he learned as a child was that the truth is there to be spoken,' Gus says. 'His father never made a lot of money. He was supported as clergy sometimes are, but not well. That is one of the ethics – for want of a better word – which he has retained from his upbringing. Selling yourself comes with compromises.'

Journalist Colin James agrees that money has rarely been a prime motivator. When it comes to money, the cold hard truth wins. 'Philip's scratched it,' James says. 'It takes balls to choose that way of life. There have been many crises in Philip's life with money.' After five decades of often successful labour in mining and media, Philip sits at his peppercorn-rented cottage, accounting for what he owns, and the first song line you think of is John Lennon's '. . . imagine no possessions'. No property. No car. No TV.

A few relatively expensive guitars. Books. Precious little else. And you could apply 'Imagine there's no heaven', the opening line of Lennon's 'Imagine', to Philip's way of thinking.

Like Lennon, Philip is no saint. Again, close friends refer to his 'dark' side, in various but persuasive ways. When they discuss his gentle, loving, kind and thoughtful impulses, they speak fondly of Sylvia, his mother. The father, right-wing pastor Jimmy White, is blackened by his shuddering violence and his sinister, controlling nature.

Yes, he provided food and shelter and education. And, on the face of it, he was a normal dad. Telling Grimm bedtime stories. But Philip, who likes to draw, paints a picture that also contains a hideous spectre. A foaming, enraged, manic street preacher bent on hurt. A father who exploded into action, thrashing his children over and over, at times on flimsy evidence of misbehaviour. A father who sold his eldest son's car, behind his back, so he wouldn't be free to roam far as he wished. A father who – chillingly – kicked his eldest son out of home and hearth on the breathless news that he had won a scholarship and was going to University of Adelaide, aged seventeen. The physical punishments left their marks on body and mind.

It is most observed by close friends like Gus Howard. 'When he's not scaring people, he's making them feel safe,' says Gus.

> When he gets on a spoken riff, he can be quite something. When I met him, he was already a wild man, a crazy poet. His everyday dialogue was also prone to be epic-yarn-rave poetry. Scary for anyone unprepared and a room stopper. Very powerful. Often in those days we were all ridiculously close together. It was fuelled by hashish or something and so was the room. But I have seen him scare strangers with his long sentences and deep voice, responding to whatever was in front of us with a wall of words tipping from him. A lot of it was from the hillbilly *Under Milk Wood* childhood he'd had and the place he'd recently escaped from. Nobody had heard those kind of sagas before. His father

was a shouter-street-corner-preacher. Philip was taken to windy streets in Murray Bridge and Adelaide and expected to do the same. Some of his utterings had a great sense of crisis.

In those days, most of the people I knew made a study of near madness. So you don't watch Philip reciting poetry. You hear him speak at length through an anecdote that goes to another plane. The poetry is in the passion, the persistent string of mind-state description, not of him, but his subjects.

You wonder how the people in his stories survived. How isolated, tragic, mad, angry, dark, sad, manic can a person be?

And you believe it. You stop thinking of yourself and wonder if anyone, anywhere, is actually sane. I know people have wondered the same thing about him, right to this day, and it can scare people.

CHAPTER 8

Women of Substance

'Philip was a very sensitive individual who was obviously checking out how the world worked, how people's relationships worked, their dynamics.'

– Ieva Kains, Mount Barker High School teacher, on her top student of 1969

The teenaged Philip and his brothers were quickly growing into strapping lads. All that fresh air, hunting and exploration. A friend who saw three of them, aged in their formidable twenties, walking down Rundle Street side-by-side, remembers a springy rural gait, wharfie chests and a big rush of fraternal unity. Terry Plane recalled a night at the British Hotel in North Adelaide, drinking jugs of vodka and orange with Philip, Stephen and Paul.

> A bloke nearby came up and kept flicking Stephen's very long hair and taunting him. Stephen eventually said: 'If you do that again, I'm going to open your face like a book. And it'll really hurt.' I reckon Stephen was the heaviest of the brothers and very strong, like their father. He turned around and grabbed the tormentor by the scruff of his jacket and shirt and lifted him off the ground with one hand and slammed him against the wall. He said, 'Listen, cunt, I told you not to do that,' and then dropped him. The guy was quivering and he and his mates drifted away.

Plane met Pastor Jimmy, once, over a cup of tea in the family kitchen.

> My impressions were all coloured by the stories Philip had told me. I looked at his father and thought, This is the bloke who staggered down the aisle with a chair on his back, pretending to be the crucified Christ, at an Easter service at Murray Bridge. Very theatrical. I could see why Philip was like he was. He had been on preaching tours with his father until he was about seventeen. I knew that Philip had been brainwashed by his father, basically. And his life from then on was a reaction to that repression. When he broke out, he broke out in a big way. He drank heavily, he was into drugs. At a party one night I walked into a room to find him rooting the host's wife. You can use that. Look, I don't think Philip would object to that. He was into everything to rebel against what his father had made him.
>
> But his mother was a very gentle soul. Lovely, lovely woman. And I think you could see that more in Andrew than Philip. I wouldn't describe Stephen or Philip or Paul as gentle, but I'd describe Andrew that way.

As they grew into their teenaged years, the White brothers took on more labouring work, building up muscle and skills. This included being hired by a couple of free-spirited lesbians who ruled the local roost in the manner of aristocratic Englishwomen. 'We learnt a lot there, the basics,' Philip says. 'How to sharpen knives, clean a shearing floor, shoot vermin, muster stock, pull weeds, dress sheep.' Philip adopts the mien of a peasant forced by social station to accept the authority of the mistress of the manor when he adds that the boys were 'allowed' to take red gum firewood from the property 'to keep our cooking stove and fireplaces fed'.

On drinkster.com, Philip writes about Nora Young. In her direct bloodline was namesake Nora Creina, daughter of Lady Charlotte Bacon. Lady Bacon was a daughter of Edward, 5th Earl of Oxford and Mortimer, and widow of the late General Bacon, a Waterloo veteran. She spent some time in Adelaide, saying the want of ceremony in colonial life made these years the happiest of her life. A not-so-distant member of this privileged family tree is reputed to have had a fling with the romantic poet Lord Byron, resulting in an illegitimate child who bore a strong resemblance to the man known as 'mad, bad and dangerous to know'.

Nora Young, says Philip, moved into Kanmantoo Station with her Beretta-machine-pistol-packing girlfriend, Ida Tate Smith.

> The eccentric kleptomaniac Alison Woosterman Howgate lived in a stylish modern cottage on their large lawns. In spite of being an expert driver of her big V8 Valiant Regal, Alison always pretended to be blind. She affected the awkward shaded spectacles worn by postwar blind folks and even kept a dribbling golden labrador in harness as a prop.
>
> On Saturdays, the expert painter Nora would run watercolour classes on the verandah, while I mowed the lawn. I couldn't imagine then why you'd have a kid mow the bloody lawn with a noisy, smelly old Victa four-stroke while you were sitting there hitting the Chestnut Teal sherry and learning how to paint, but I imagine it had something to do with proving one was sufficiently well orf to run staff. They were mainly khaki-jodhpur short-back-and-sides lasses at those genteel soirées. Not a sherry head, Nora would stir heaps of brown sugar into dark rum in a huge grandpa's teacup and lap it noisily with a teaspoon. She chain-smoked Alpine filters and spoke with a toasted Tom Waits timbre.
>
> It was a cool but crazy place to live, Kanmantoo in the fifties and sixties: there weren't many farming villages anywhere else whose aristocracy was an openly gay matriarchy.

In the meantime, Philip was glad when his family shifted from the outer edges of Kanmantoo into the village, having felt isolated in the old shepherd's cottage with its four rooms. As usual, nothing was simple for the Whites, given Mum and Dad's fervour for hard-nosed religion. The next home was in what started out as the Black Dog Inn, built in 1856 in the midst of a copper-mine boom. It closed its doors very soon after and became a residence.

'Dad had to exorcise the demons before we could move in,' Philip said. God's gaze was everywhere. According to his English teacher at Mount Barker High, Philip was interested in theatre. Ieva Kains, who encountered Philip in his matriculation year in 1969, remembers he played guitar in *Bye Bye Birdie* and was the Tramp in her production of the play *Salad Days*. Philip wasn't able to attend Ieva's drama camps, despite his enthusiasm.

> I gather from talking to him [many years later] his parents didn't want him to be doing such non-religious activities. It's interesting to me how he actually managed to get away to rehearse. Kanmantoo was quite a hike from Mount Barker by school bus, twenty kilometres or more.
>
> He was in a lot of sports things at school; he was in a soccer team. We rehearsed intensively, so how he managed to get away from home, I don't know. It sounded like Father had the rules down pat and you did what Father said.
>
> Philip was a very sensitive individual who was obviously checking out how the world worked, how people's relationships worked, their dynamics. He and his fellow students were so well behaved, they sat and they were courteous. It was only much later, when he got in touch with me, when he talked to me about his early life, I realised I had been introducing him to influences he wasn't getting at home.
>
> His wonderful command of English does come from the St James Bible, beautiful cadences. English is a language which, when it is spoken well, is absolutely magnificent. I taught the

> English curriculum slightly differently to the traditional teaching and I think this appealed to Philip. It was unique material taught in a unique way. Philip was my top student. I heard he was writing and publishing and was a wine writer. I have to say I wasn't surprised. Because his writing had been terrific.

Ieva and her outstanding student met thirty-seven years later. The adult version of the student displayed a compassion and supply of emotional support that several other friends have noted with admiration. 'Philip helped me psychologically – I was in a bit of a downward spiral after my husband died,' Ieva says.

> Philip had been trying to find me and, finally, wrote to the president of the Latvian Federation, a friend of mine. Seven degrees of separation for Latvians, I don't think so! Then when he started writing to me, it was all very flattering, lovely stuff. Encouraged me to think more, read more, again. Psychologically, it was like a gin and tonic. He made me feel worthwhile as a thinking human being. You can imagine. Here's me, a silver-haired widow, and a student says, 'Can I take you out for lunch?' I mean, how good is that?
>
> Trust me, that is really good for one's ego. After your closest loved one dies, you become vulnerable, a non-person. You're not special to anybody – even though I know my family – children, grandchildren, extended – love me.

Asked how he did overall at school, Philip replied: 'Depended on the teacher. If the teacher was a fool I failed. The first time I did Matric, I was second in the State in English and failed the other four subjects because the teachers didn't inspire me. I did Matric again, and got straight As and a scholarship.'

It was with a heady purpose that Philip walked from the Kanmantoo store to his family home at the former Black Dog

Inn, now apparently free of evil spirits thanks to Pastor Jimmy's exorcism. 'I've got my matriculation certificate. I'm full of pride. Dad's sitting there and he has his eleven o'clock cup of tea in his hand, waiting for me to return with the bread and the milk and the mail.'

Pastor Jimmy asks his firstborn: 'What's that you've got?'

'Oh, I've matriculated and I've got a scholarship.'

Dad: 'What are you going to do?'

'I think I'll go to university.'

Dad: 'Well you can get out now. That's a Communist training camp.'

Philip sniggers as if embarrassed by such an outburst of paternal scorn. 'And that was it. So no money. No support.' His mesmerising oratory, for just a demi-minute in the conversation, shakes.

> It wasn't a surprise, because that was what he was like. But I still didn't expect it, though I should have. I didn't go back there much for several years. Dad died four or five years ago, just before Mum. We had a very competitive relationship when I became an adult. Because we were both in the preaching business, really. He was working for God and I was working for Satan. And I can guarantee you I got a lot more than he ever f–n got. He was envious of my audience. My congregation was much bigger than his, through newspapers and television. But it gave him a sort of pride in me.
>
> Like Mum used to say: 'Aw, our boy's a celebrity.' Dad would say: 'Nah, he's just a sinner, an anti-Christ.'

CHAPTER 9

Leaving the Nest

'I hung out there like a gutter rat.'
– Philip on his early days at University of Adelaide

The holy and unholy war had escalated between Pastor Jimmy and Philip, his eldest son. It was God versus the Devil at fifty paces. At the age of seventeen, Philip sensed the fighting – literally and metaphorically – was reaching a climax. One of the first indicators was his strong and insolent response to his dad selling his first car behind his back – at a profit.

> That was the old man showing me that I shouldn't go anywhere. So I'd just gone to Cooktown in Queensland and sent him a postcard. I was taunting him now. And he soon realised that I could go anyway. That there was no point in being a prick like he was. I had to become a rebel because it was my responsibility as the firstborn to get out of the house and stop costing them so much money. And setting a bad example for my little brothers, because I was worldly.

The ticket out of Kanmantoo into the big city lay in the hands of a slightly older man, a member of Pastor Jimmy's congregation.

> Graham was a bloke who used to attend our church and drove up from Adelaide to Murray Bridge every Sunday. Always had a girlfriend with a Bible on her lap. And he always had the hottest car. The fastest cars. He was, like, my mate. I'd been to Sydney

and Melbourne with him. My parents trusted him enough to let me go with him – because he carried a Bible, so he must be safe [puffs on a pipe, coughs, laughs]. So, when I ran away from home, I rented a room from Graham in his house at Holden Hill.

Philip was well aware he'd be leaving behind a streak of adolescent fun that wouldn't be tolerated in Adelaide. Such as the 130-mph [200 kph] drag races between Murray Bridge and Callington featuring one car filled with beer and the other laden with Bibles (the Bibles won). Fellow university students mocked the hillbilly from the north-eastern suburb, 'the implication being my mum and dad didn't have a house in Walkerville'. Making new friends who weren't so stuck-up was important to this intransigent country lad with visions of becoming a master of abstracts – a poet, artist, musician and writer.

I made friends very quickly, including Zing Hai Tan, who won the Tennyson Medal for English when I came second. He taught me about Chinese food (and later founded a market research company).

Philip wasn't one to waste time on fake airs and graces. What you first see and hear is what you get, to this day. 'I hung out there like a gutter rat,' he says of his early days at uni.

Used to be able to get long cigarette butts because the rich kids would only smoke a bit of a cigarette and then go to their lectures, so you could grab them. That's where I met John Kingsmill – picking up butts. He was pretending to be poor and I was wishing I was rich.

Graphic designer Kingsmill and Philip later worked together on independent magazines like the *Adelaide Preview* and *Adelaide Review*.

Another new mate came in a most stylish package. 'Nick Lainas was Greek; had black hair just so, a beautiful leather jacket, Carnaby Street shirt, a real dude, you know,' Philip recalls, fingers sliding softly over his own collar. Fashionable, well-made clothes were a part of the sensuous world for Philip.

> I encountered Nick very early at university, and he had a little bit of money. He took me to the Windsor and showed me things like the best movies of the time. He'd been living in England for a couple of years, just checking out the music and working in the government.

For all the excitement of the new and fascinating in Adelaide, Philip was soon restless. He studied English, history, politics and philosophy, and had won a Commonwealth Scholarship worth $500, a fair slab of money in the early seventies. 'I didn't like philosophy much. I didn't meet any great philosophers at Adelaide Uni.' Then there was the spectre of a call-up to go fight for his country in the Vietnam War.

> I had to leave Adelaide Uni because of the draft. The way it worked was if you hadn't registered and your birthdate didn't roll out of the marble bag, they let you go as a low priority. But, if your ball rolled and you hadn't registered, they were knocking on your father's door in weeks looking for you. Jail. For the duration of your national service. I was facing the reality that I'd probably have to hide. University became less important to me, and I'd only been there for one year. When I went into hiding, the people around me looked after me: Verity Lawton and Rob Brookman and John Kingsmill. I was allowed to sleep on their couches.
>
> I knew there were ASIO spies watching us; Commonwealth Police, plainclothed on campus, picking up draft dodgers and people who hadn't registered. Some of them we knew. Every time we set foot on campus we were in enemy territory.

> I got by on very little money. But I was fortunate because I was a little bit known as a poet, this mysterious long-haired bloke from the country who wrote lyric poetry and appeared in poetry circles.

Poetry has always been close under the skin, making it an irritant and a salve. 'I write poetry when the moment comes,' Philip says. 'It's not a specific aim. I'll be thinking about something and a line will emerge. I'll write it down and then build around it – it usually doesn't take long.' The art is not separate from the rest of his writing. 'You could cut up some of my wine reviews and rearrange the paragraphs and they would look and sound like poems.'

On a visit to Adelaide for the 1972 Writers' Week festival, Lawrence Ferlinghetti, New York experimental and beat poet and social activist, predicted Philip White might be the next big thing in Australian verse. In the eighties, Philip made friends with Les Murray, via Christopher Pearson, who ran the arts magazine the *Adelaide Review*. Philip has fond memories of the man who would become known as Australia's greatest poet:

> He chain-smoked cigars, which affected his delivery, made it wheezy and puffy, very short of breath. I saw him once, egg on his chin, wearing that great big stripey jumper. I think I learned that he was entrapped by poetry. It was his enemy, couldn't get away from it, couldn't stop. Otherwise, he would have been a dairy farmer.

The two men shared a disdain for fluffy niceties. One instance that draws Philip's wicked, gargled laugh came in 1993, when Murray was describing the oath of allegiance as 'heavy and pompous and sort of farting with sincerity'. Just the man to fix the problem? Not quite, as it turned out, when the larrikin poet was officially invited to make changes. Murray ran a line, 'And I expect to be true to Australia, as I expect her to be true to me.' The second half of that sentence was cut, much to the author's disgust. 'Les was really pissed off that Prime Minister John Howard cut it,' Philip says. 'Why should I, the citizen, have to affirm any bloody thing towards the nation?' Murray asked, conceding his wording was 'a bit more daring. It put the citizen above the government, and made the government into our servants . . .'

Nonetheless, the friendship did not translate to Philip getting his work published in *Quadrant*, the magazine edited by Murray, who had asked to be sent poems he'd heard recited. 'I sent him the ones he liked and some more and within a week they came back with a note: 'We won't need any of these, thank you.' Star winemaker Chris Carpenter, based in California, has had a Whitey poem hanging on his office wall for a couple of years. Philip recalls:

> Before, it made no sense to him; he could never work out what it meant. Even to me, as I was writing, it was a series of riddles. It often happens that it'll all come together – even for the poet – after months or years. I didn't know what it meant beyond the theme of death. It's about life being the fulcrum we need to make this lever work to prepare us for death.

We only come here to die. 'Wipe your tears on your sleeve, my waif . . .' It's an elderly person advising a young person at a graveside. 'Chris rang not long ago, and said the poem suddenly made sense to him.'

Training oneself to leave

As the dead become accustomed
to the other side of all we thought

was permanent it's cool to watch
their rage subside without them once
considering forgiveness. They
concentrate on other things, soon
realising this living bit was fickle
and really only necessary to give
fulcrum to the lever that was
in their hands before they even
came here to train themselves
to leave. So wipe your tears on
your sleeve, my waif, take one
last look in the hole, check your
young palms for blisters and go
live hungrily among the sisters.

While the Commonwealth Scholarship was generous, it had too many restrictions for a young man with a lust for knowledge. 'In retrospect I wish I'd done town planning. But it would've been too early to have set my brain in that direction anyway.' Philip's final act signified a stubborn reluctance to compromise and a desire to stick his neck out; damn the consequences to comfort or career. It would be a lifelong trait.

> I wrote my English paper. It was a letter to the examiner, ignoring the question and suggesting: You shouldn't be asking me this. You should be asking me about Vietnam, about drug culture. I wrote a cry of passion to whoever marked the paper. It went to a lovely old lecturer called Dita Russell, who looked a bit like Valmai Hankel [awarded an AM 'for significant service to library and information services and the wine industry, as a writer']

with short hair, one of those grand old academic, Anglican bluestocking types. I got a beautiful letter from her to visit and have a talk. She was very concerned. Asked me what was I going to do next? I said I'd probably go and get work somewhere else. That all rolled on and I went back to Kanmantoo, rented a cottage and worked at the mine.

CHAPTER 10

Pieces of Peace

'A whole lot of preachers came from Ireland to Australia for work experience, and stayed with us. None of them could preach, but they were very good with a rifle.' – Philip

For Philip's part, he will claim he has made his peace with the domestic horrors of home in Kanmantoo. But that is not always reflected in his comments. As he speaks of this, magpies are softly carolling on the deep-green grassy grounds of his latest home, at the Yangarra Estate Vineyard at Kangarilla, south of Adelaide and roughly 45 minutes' drive from the CBD. The view is so easy on the eye, so lazily comfortable, so far and wide with simple beauty, it is hard to connect with Philip's next words. 'I watched him f–n die,' he says of his father, Pastor Jimmy White.

> Yelling out for help and no Jesus there to help him through the pearly gates. My brothers and I are probably more angry about him now than when he was alive. We're being more honest about what he was really like: a violent bully. He used Jesus as a threat like [Cardinal] George Pell does, in a way.
>
> My father and the Reverend Ian Paisley were friends. I met Paisley. He was a very scary big bloody Protestant bullyboy terrorist. Killer. Awful person. I went through a ceremony when I was fourteen, made you swear to kill Catholics. Where you would swear on the Bible, in the dark, in this room at home, that you would kill Catholics if the Lord wanted you to. I thought it

> was all bullshit. A whole lot of preachers came from Ireland to Australia for work experience, and stayed with us. None of them could preach, but they were very good with a rifle. Very good hunters.
>
> One night we had a party. The balloons started going off, popping. I was watching this priest from Belfast, and I said to my old man: 'He's got shell shock – he's not a preacher.' My old man realised I knew these blokes weren't priests, they were terrorists who had to get out of Ireland. He was directly involved in the Troubles. Farmers on the Eyre Peninsula, even in times of drought, would give their ten per cent tithe to Paisley. So Paisley had to come out here every few years to say his thank you.

There can be little doubt Jimmy White had a major flaw in that he regarded the first part of the Bible as a working manual rather than a set of stories with a horrific bent. Yet he could just as quickly be seen as an everyday father, looking out for his boys and their futures. One example was Jimmy's courting of the copper mine at Kanmantoo. As Philip tells it:

> He was a reliable sort of dude in the sense that he was the local preacher, and became involved as the night watchman. It suited him perfectly because he could sit in the ute and read the Bible all night, and write sermons. So he gradually got all his sons work. To take us off his hands for a bit. Because we were a handful. Yeah. Borrowed his car and used up all his petrol. So, almost inadvertently, he set his sons on a career route. I worked in the office. I knew all about rock collection, lease law, how to record and store rock samples. I was always interested in natural history, rock formations and waterfalls and road cuttings.

It is reportedly rare to hear a Philip yarn that does not surprise or otherwise amaze. Typically striking is Philip's explanation of how the mine had to shut down in the early seventies. That was triggered by the rise in the copper-rich Chile of Salvador Allende, in 1970 the first Marxist to be elected to the national presidency of a liberal democracy. Allende went after the American interests in the lucrative mines, making them liable for damages to the State. Hefty deductions included charges for 'loans invested poorly' and 'excessive profits'. Philip takes up the story, supported by the public record.

> Mining at Kanmantoo was so marginal that it was only viable for the duration of the closure of the biggest mine in the world, in Chile. Allende had promised he would shut down the mine (and others) until its American owners and operators brought in health and safety restrictions, as they had to have in the US mines. Up until then peasants in bare feet were getting killed underground.
>
> But the Americans didn't want that, because they were at war in Vietnam and they needed copper. So Henry Kissinger sent in the CIA and they overthrew Allende in 1973. Their mines came back into play and forced the shutdown at Kanmantoo. One of my jobs was to watch the world copper prices on the Telex, from the intelligence agencies paid by the miners themselves.

Here is an example of the world's truth merging seamlessly with Philip's view of events. And, in general, he has a dynamic, genuine connection to the facts.

That has not always been the case, as even good friends and lovers attest. Somewhere, sometimes, Philip's appetite for the truth gets subverted, and the people on the receiving end of his versions make no secret of their disappointment, or sometimes anger and anguish.

Gus Howard tackles the question of whether Philip can be a fabulist in a negative sense, in light of Mark Thomson's more forgiving assessment, which is that his friend is a fabulist in the best possible sense, one who has always expected the world to be more fabulous than it is. Gus:

> Philip reminds me of Phillip Adams when I hear Adams talk about how he invented the Australian film industry. Yes, it is mis-remembering as an art form. This is the one thing that disappoints me most about him, and I don't mean it's personal disappointment, because he wouldn't be who he is without his great ability to interpret. But I wish he could have made a quite good living out of fiction, because he really understands fiction and storytelling very well. And, occasionally he will exaggerate or mis-remember or fictionalise something in order to make a point.
>
> It is a pity he never found a solid career in solid, legitimate fiction. So that his life could be turned into a work of imagination, legitimately. There are many times when his life gets turned into the work of imagination kind of illegitimately because that's the way his mind works.

It is pointless and dangerous to make simplistic comparisons where Philip White is concerned. Slap one label on him and it will make a fool of the labeller. A lit-up, fizzing example is provided by a long-term lover who was upset by grapevine rustling that Philip had been unfaithful. 'He never promised me he would be faithful,' she recollects. 'What he did do was not talk about any of that, and I made it clear that monogamy was of prime importance.' Professional photographer Milton Wordley knows the light and the dark:

> He's a genuinely good friend and a person who has a few issues that he deals with really well. He's very open with the people he knows that he's got a few things going on. A lot of them are

to do with having been beaten up and concussions. I've seen the neurologist's report and Philip's been knocked unconscious many times. He's got the same thing as the American gridiron players. We know how he drinks, as well, so how he can still concentrate to write is beyond me.

An illustration of his personality came when we were out at a small restaurant one night and Philip was making his customary use of colourful language. Effing and blinding. A chap came up to our table and said, 'Look, we're sitting near you with young children and we're Christians and we'd really like you to ask your friend to stop swearing.' Philip was so upset by the realisation that he'd caused such discomfort that he had to go outside, crying, and virtually hug a tree. On the other hand, it might have been a completely different reaction had there been someone in that group he didn't like. He could be acerbic.

What drew me to Philip was his genuine outstanding skill as a writer, his knowledge of things. One day, when my partner Anne-Marie's mother was alive, we were having lunch at T-Chow and Philip walked in and I asked him to join us. Anne-Marie wasn't all that sure about it because Philip can be outlandish and outspoken. After he left, Anne-Marie was concerned her mother might have been upset by some of the language. And her mum was a 78-year-old Sunday-School-teaching, cardigan-wearing woman who you wouldn't think would warm to Philip. But her mum said, 'What a fascinating man. I haven't enjoyed lunch with anybody for so long.'

If a broad brushstroke were to be made over a portrait of Philip, say a flourish of country music star Johnny Cash, few would protest. Cash was a man of several bony angles. A God-fearing man who transgressed in rapid-fire fashion. Was madly in love with his wife, June Carter Cash, yet was serially unfaithful. Took massive amounts of drugs. Openly admitted that he'd probably been more 'bad' than 'good' for long periods – both of which coincided with falling off the wagon. But when it came to the truth, as in the inviolable sanctity of his core beliefs, he walked the line. The straight and steady line. Even when it was difficult to see in the fog of real life.

There is a theory that Philip has always had his eye on darkness. He himself has indicated his father may well have been trying to thrash the 'wickedness' from his son, who had taken sides with the Devil, against his father's faith in God. While Pastor Jimmy tried to save the drunks in the street, his son was thinking: 'They're having a lot more fun than me – and that became very alluring.'

Gus Howard, who chose not to follow a path that might have led him to the priesthood, believes his great friend is on a search for *why* there is darkness. 'You're trying to find out what is this bloody darkness anyway,' Gus says. 'Why does it scare everybody, and why am I attracted to it and scared of it at the same time?'

There are two kinds of truth. One that deals in cold hard facts. The other is one that is held regardless of the hurt, pain and disadvantage it brings down on the holder. Philip says he gave grudging respect for his father's predictability, in that 'you always knew when he was going to hit you'.

Truth is not necessarily a light. It can be a darkness. Constant, undying, reliable and predictable darkness. Much of Philip's poetry was focused on his childhood, particularly his father's always simmering streak of violence.

Pastor James's Heart Attack

When the bloke hands you the fish'n'chips
He does it coolly over his till,
Takes the money, slides the drawer,
And gets bloody close to the correct change
Without once taking his eyes off the street outside.

After nilly eighty years of fat, salt, starch and sugar,
My Old Man's in the Royal Adelaide with a
dodgy pump;
Scared enough to put away his ancient fear
Of letting humans interfere in God's Big Plan to
Come down from the hills in an ambulance,
Take their advice and let 'em put in a pacemaker.

Pacemaker? Gazing sideways like a fishmonger at
The reflection in that hospital window,
I got Wyatt Earp riding through the chest of
My Father The Preacher,
Who's lying there like somebody's just handed him
his Last Fish,
When this Pisces Dutch fishing sheila I love
– 'Who was that Raven-Haired Beauty?'
he asked when she'd gone –
Anyway she walks in for the first time beside me
With fresh fish on her breath and my sperm on
her hands,

He goes a sort of dishwater grey as his
blood remembers,
And he's kicking his sheets.

After a long careful gaze of this,
She looks at me like her ice cream's jumped
Off its cone into the forty-plus gutter,
And sees me become that old bastard:
Scared and jittery, lustful and fucked:
A rotting king, flat on his silver back.

No chance of fresh black feathers on that helmet.

Pastor Jimmy puts his trust in The Lord,
Whispers prayers over the phone
To Sylvia my mother each morning
While she kneels with a Bible in her hand
On a mattress on the floor in my attic
Just over the street from the heart ward.

She sleeps as close to sin as she's got for sixty
years those nights,
Near the bed where I'm sliding silently into
my fishy raven,
Whispering about orgasms.

Wondering how many you can get.

Pastor James gets better with his new electric ticker
– Having put an end to his jealousy of his wife,
Who'd sprach too eagerly of the food at my place –
Takes her back to The Purple Valley and goes
on with it.
She's been a bit of a raven in her day, mind you.
Still is, under the fat and the tangled feathers.

After I introduced her to a slimy mate,
My raven went off to Sydney on whoring work
And everything's settled down nicely.
Sometimes, when she's back here resting,
She does the same shit with her eyes as
the fish'n'chip bloke.

Philip White

CHAPTER 11

Rivers of Beer

'I probably paid Philip in beer. Most of the time we couldn't pay people. Christopher Pearson used to write book reviews and I'd pay him in Cooper's Ale.' – Terry Plane, journalist

Adelaide had a bit of a swing about it as it sauntered into the 1970s. Still punched above its weight as the third city behind Sydney and Melbourne. The mood was more laidback; carefree. The cost of living was not so onerous. A person could take a few bold chances with work. Not so much a career path, more a downhill run in a homemade go-cart, with experimental twists and turns.

And so it was with Terry Plane, a boy from Wallaroo, a port and old copper mining town north-west of Adelaide. His interests intersected perfectly with those of Philip White – music, cars, literature, fine food and wine. And, lest they be regarded as simply good-time Charlies, it must be said they shared a deep care for the environment that was not as widespread as it is today. In the seventies, Plane co-edited with Colin Talbot an environmentally flavoured magazine, *Saving Grace*. The content was low-key – gardening, composting and growing to eat, as well as references to air pollution and the negatives of plastic waste. That lasted all of two months, but a seed was planted.

Back in Adelaide, he was managing a few bands. One of them,

Dona Nobis, wrote a song about global warming when it was a much smaller issue than it is today. 'The lyrics were about icebergs melting and sea levels rising,' Plane said, looking back in fond awe at two of the founding members, Peter and Marin Doley.

> Then I decided to start this monthly magazine, *Adelaide Preview*. The driving force behind it was a friend, Kym Krummel – he and his brother were running Mothers Bookshop off Coromandel Place. His idea was to preview all the new book releases, which would obviously help sales.
>
> And I said why don't we expand it to cover music and theatre, sport, all sorts of things?

Enter Philip, stage left, soon after the first edition. At the time, Terry recalls, Philip was a public servant with the Mines Department. He rang up saying he wanted to write about music, records and live shows. 'I thought, interesting bloke,' Plane says.

> We had an entertaining initial chat. Just from the way he spoke, his turn of phrase, I thought there was a chance he could write. So I said, 'Show me what you can do.' The stuff came in and it was beautiful. His writing is beautifully descriptive; he is a very entertaining writer.

The tall and rangy newcomer had that rarity, a voice. It cannot be taught, bought or wrought. In the May 1978 edition, Philip confesses to trying hard to ignore the Sex Pistols. That vow turned inside out when he heard 'Anarchy In The UK'. He wrote:

> It came out of the good old ABC radio late at night, took the shape of a 90-volt cattle prod in the room before me, turned itself up to frazzle and bloody assaulted me. *HAHAHAHAHA! . . . 'cause I wanna be ANARCHY.*
>
> A growing force which picked its snotty nose in the face of *Vogue*-ridden Jaggers, Bowies and Stewarts.

The Pistols 'broke all the rules' of the music industry. 'They beat the shit out of it, raped it, crucified it, tore it to shreds and then pumped it through the airwaves like napalm.' Not much journalism survives intact after more than forty years, especially not in the realm of rock. Philip notes excellent songwriter and bassist Glen Matlock got cast out of the band for liking the Beatles.

> His replacement, Sid Vicious, 'never really noticed the bass, couldn't tell it from a piano . . . I got the job because I beat up Nick Kent [legendary scribe for *New Musical Express*].'

Who can say with precision what forges writers? Of W.B. Yeats, it was said, 'Ireland hurt him into poetry'. No doubt, natural ability played a role in shaping Philip.

As to his direct influences, Philip is sure of one comparison: 'Don't dare call me Hunter S. Thompson.'

> I used to get a bit annoyed when people likened me to Hunter. I'm sure he had an influence on me as far as bravado goes, and risqué behaviour. But I didn't like being likened to him too much, and I still don't. Probably the first non-Christian writer I really got to enjoy as a journalist (I wasn't allowed to read *Time* magazine, for example) was Ralph J. Gleason. I loved reading his stuff and when the Band played a concert at the Fillmore and he reviewed it, I thought, Wow, got to hear those people.

Meanwhile, Philip was on a road less travelled. The kind of place on the map he prefers as part of avoiding the madding crowds. (There is a legend that the Saturday Table guests at T-Chow in Adelaide's Chinatown have heard the more mature Philip – more than once – complain there are too many people in attendance when the number rises above ten.)

Philip was looking towards Europe.

I was most influenced as a writer, probably, by the American expatriates in Paris between the wars. I was living with Maire Mannik. She was a *New Yorker* magazine fan; she introduced me to people like Pauline Kael, the film critic, who I loved. I've still got bound copies of all her film reviews.

Those writers who were in Paris – Paris was good to them because the franc was worth nothing between the wars and on their meagre income, they could live quite well. So you had F. Scott Fitzgerald, who was rich.

But there were all those other interesting people like Waverley Root, Joe Liebling [A.J. Liebling], Janet Flanner. I ended up searching out bound copies of their works. In a sense, a lot of my language is American–English influenced by French culture.

As much as Philip is an acclaimed writer, those who know him well speak in awe of his powers of oratory, such as when he tells great stories in his favourite pubs. Not all that many have heard of A.J. Liebling, but Philip makes you feel you've just spent the last hour chatting with him.

Joe Liebling was an interesting character. He was a boxer in New York who got too fat to box because he was a bit of a trencherman. So he became a boxing writer. He ended up getting fired because he gave too many failed betting tips to his publisher. So Liebling, this corpulent fellow in a boater wearing a sandwich board proclaiming 'Hire Joe Liebling', is walking up and down the street outside newspaper offices. A lad comes up with a business card from Harold Ross, editor of the *New Yorker*. Harold said: 'I like your writing. There's going to be a war, would you cover it for me?' Joe's coverage of WWII is the best, amazing.

Over the decades, the Kanmantoo Kid has remained typical

of many gifted writers, protecting his words with a ferocity unsettling to the inexperienced sub-editor. Even in his formative stages, learning to fly, he was no pushover. Michael Zerman got a close-up of the consequences when he was helping redesign *Adelaide Preview* magazine. A problem arose in a review of Blondie's 'In The Flesh', with the author making no secret of his primal attraction to lead singer Debbie Harry.

Women's underwear featured in the last paragraph. 'I suggested I'd crawl a full lap of the Berlei factory through broken glass on bare knees to see her sing it live,' Philip recalls. Mortified by what he saw as sexist, Zerman cut the final paragraph. Later came a loud banging on the front door of his home in Hackney. 'It was one of those 1890s cottages with a big banger,' Zerman says. 'And the only other time it had gone off that loudly was when the coppers came around looking for pot. I opened the door and there was Philip, completely furious. I wasn't particularly scared – I was more surprised.'

Philip was in full, indignant flight: 'The Debbie Harry review. You cut out my last paragraph. Why did you do that?' Zerman replied, 'I didn't like it. It was pretty sexist and offensive.' And Philip yelled: 'Who gives you the right to cut my fucking copy?' Zerman spat back a mouthful and slammed the door in Philip's face.

Today, there are conflicting versions of what actually happened more than forty years ago. But no one denies the essence of that confrontation, which is an example supported by others who later had to whittle Philip's words. The incident quickly blew over. 'In retrospect, it was naughty of me to have made that cut,' Zerman says. 'Luckily, Philip is not a person to hold a grudge. He's a generous man.'

While passions ran high, rewards were low. The *Adelaide Preview* may well have been a dynamic nursery for nascent

talent, especially compared to the then-sober morning *Advertiser* newspaper. But it was not exactly a river of gold. Those with workplace sensitivities – like Occupational Health & Safety and fair wage standards – should look away now. Pay often came in the form of beer. Sure, purists might argue, it was Coopers Ale, but it wasn't cash. Brought a new meaning to drinking away all your wages. Such under-the-bar-counter labour hire would cause apoplexy today. Yet no one got hurt. It was simply a sign of the experimental, freewheeling times that freelancers were more than willing partners in the wheeze. Real gold lay up ahead, hopefully.

Plane, who has had a long, distinguished career in journalism, thinks back: 'I probably paid Philip in beer. Most of the time we couldn't pay people. Christopher Pearson used to write book reviews and I'd pay him in Cooper's Ale, and I suspect it was the same with Philip.'

The assistant editor was Dennis Atkins, beginning a career in political journalism while also writing the Possum's Pages of the *Sunday Mail*. Plane reckons Atkins had left the *Adelaide Preview* by the time he asked Philip to take over what was an ailing operation. 'He did two editions and it went broke.' While Philip was always on time with his copy, the same could not be said of the late Christopher Pearson, who went on to be a well-regarded publisher of *Preview*'s more durable progeny, the *Adelaide Review*. 'I was always going round banging on his door at his Wellington Square apartment, saying we need the book reviews now,' Plane recalls. 'And Pearson would say: "More Coopers Ale." I'd go and get him more beer.'

Sadly, the *Adelaide Review* is no more, having been killed off in September 2020. Founded in 1984 by a young Mark Jamieson from a small office at 13 Hindley Street, the weekly was taken over by one of the contributors, Pearson. He was a divisive figure who tended to polarise opinion as to his character – his merry band of intensely loyal admirers and followers on one side. Former Foreign Affairs Minister Alexander Downer described him as 'one of the defining intellectuals of our age'. Critics saw him as a self-indulgent stooge for the right.

There can be little doubt that – in its heyday of the eighties and nineties – the *Review* was a thorn in the side of the *Advertiser.* Journalist Christian Kerr wrote for the Sydney version – a testament to the national influence of an independent from Adelaide. He says:

> It boosted careers and, despite Christopher's own ideological evolution, included such well known right-wing death beasts as Hugh Stretton, Don Dunstan and Peter Ward as key contributors for many years. There were also the long-running anti-Rupert contributions of David Bowman. It was also a crucial place to advertise if you wanted to suggest you had something special to offer. Even being a distribution point came with some cachet. The *Review* was a remarkable demonstration of cultural capital that should have been able to power on.

Plane has kept in touch with Philip, and possibly knows him as well as anyone.

> It is impossible to sum up Philip in a few words, but I love that line of Kris Kristofferson's. 'He was a walking contradiction/ Partly fact and partly fiction.' In a funny sort of way, Philip is still an Old Testament boy. Because what went into his brain in those first seventeen years is still there. Not related to Christianity, but related to everything else he does in his life. Who is he more like – his mother or his father? Father.

CHAPTER 12

Musical Influencers

'He's more Keith Richards than Mick Jagger, that's for sure.'
– David Sly

By the time Philip was twenty-one, he had created a foggy distance between himself and the stifling right-wing religious indoctrination at home. The year 1973 was one marked by more breaking of the red-hot chains. The preacher's eldest son was devouring the permissive society, tossing the gnawed bones over his shoulder. Booze. Drugs. Women. Pedals to the metal.

If music was heard within the four walls of the family home at Kanmantoo, it would have been mainly of the religious, hymnal sort. Philip has long since listened to anything and everything. At first he let his inner hillbilly rip with country music, usually from America. Gram Parsons wasn't exactly a lookalike, but you can see a resemblance in photos of both men in their twenties. Gram, who died of drug toxicity aged twenty-six, featured in The Byrds and The Flying Burrito Brothers. Commander Cody and His Lost Planet Airmen. The Grateful Dead and Steely Dan.

Philip's love for Little Feat – a high-class country rock outfit – bordered on the obsessive, according to Terry Plane. Especially after Philip met mainstay Lowell George when the band played Festival Hall in Adelaide in 1976. The ripple-soled boy from the Hills seized the chance to show Lowell around – so enthusiastically, the American expressed a desire to buy property here.

Philip admits riding around with Lowell was not all fun – the gifted guitarist was close to 140 kilograms and already suffering from binge eating, alcoholism and dropping speedballs of heroin and cocaine. But his admiration for the Californian – who at thirty-four died of a heart attack thought to have been caused by an accidental cocaine overdose – was undiminished.

Lowell was tepid about mainstream pop; he leaned towards West Coast jazz exponents like Mose Allison. That attitude was not lost on Philip, who was keen to test the possibilities of music, and not simply obey its Tin Pan Alley imperatives. One of Philip's favourite teachers, Ieva Kains, remembers introducing a range of different music to her students at Mount Barker High.

> This is what seems to have struck his imaginative faculties because there would not, for example, have been classical music at home – more church music and hymns. I played them Beethoven for teaching them about theme. I also introduced them to music such as Bob Dylan. When I was at university, a lot of my friends introduced me to jazz and folk and that seemed to have had an incredible impression on Philip.

Now, in the Spotify age, all bets are off. Once-distant stars in the musical galaxy can be summoned for a few dollars a week. Or, for free. One of Philip's recent favourites is Iggy Pop's radio show on BBC Radio 6, *Iggy Confidential* – 'a sonic cocktail' plus anecdotes.

He's always swayed to the blues: John Lee Hooker, Elmore James. By the time the Rolling Stones toured the *Exile On Main St* double album in 1973, Philip was thirsting to find out how far the lads had taken the pure blues from the first half of the twentieth century. The news around their arrival in Australia provides a taste of the social mood. The band was at the height of its creativity and jet-set decadence. Concert fans all over the United States had been rioting. Keith Richards was in the depths of a serious heroin haze. Mick Jagger's drug convictions had him on the banned list until then Immigration Minister Al Grassby relented. To have given Jagger a bad name and to have hanged him would have been 'immoral and un-Australian'.

Philip was there for one of two concerts at Memorial Drive in February – the first of which saw mini-riots and twenty-one arrests, with one police officer injured. But all he was interested in was the Jumpin' Jack Flash show. 'The full moon came up behind the stage out of the gum trees. You could hear that click as Keith plugged in his Telecaster and then Mick said, "G'day, sports."'

Philip the fan was steeping himself in all sorts. It's true his musical achievements have been less widely catalogued than his wine writing. But he must have been a handy guitarist for Paul Kelly to sneak in an informal audition. Back before the Coloured Girls and hits like 'To Her Door'. Journalist David Sly recalls hearing Philip in action when they played together at a couple of wine shows. 'He's more Keith Richards than Mick Jagger, that's for sure,' Sly says.

> As a guitarist – again, feel. He's not trying to play a million notes, not trying to dazzle people with licks, like a guitar-shop guy. Philip's all about trying to extract feel out of it, so slow, porch music. It all points to some form of artistry. You think about his poetry, his writing, his wine knowledge, his music, everything is about expression.

Gus Howard was in an early band featuring Philip on guitar.

'He and I playing music together was like the hand in the glove,' Gus recalls.

> He stood in front of me when we played and we just connected. That's when we really got to love each other because we were so complementary and willing to take chances together, we became a good outfit.

And while the band was quite successful, its progress was hampered by one of the heroin plagues that sporadically afflicted Adelaide in the seventies and eighties, and beyond. 'Made it bloody difficult, having three junkies in the band. They lost their sense of generosity.'

Philip enjoyed pursuits that are – in the main – solitary. Poetry. Drawing. Writing. Up on stage, with a band, he brought a little of that aloofness. As David Sly says, he was more Keef than Mick when it came to performance. More the steady linesman laying down that irresistible rhythm. Philip's bravado and swagger, strangely enough, were peacock feathers reserved for his wide-ranging, occasionally mesmerising bursts of plain old oratory at the Exeter.

Philip loved bands with a rich interplay, full of instruments that silkily, seamlessly folded into one another. As in Little Feat, who were at the other end of the funhouse spectrum dominated by, say, Alice Cooper or Iggy and the Stooges. What he loved was not strutting and posing, but hitting that invisible musical mark of joyous togetherness. Philip explains:

> It's more about playing with other people rather than the exposure of performance. I love the interaction with people and between the minds, especially if you're a jamming band. The subliminal tuning of the brain. I've got goosebumps just now, thinking about how cool it is when you've got a really good bass

and drums and rhythm section and you're in tune with each other. You are waiting for each other to take adventurous steps and you make available an opportunity for the other player to have a go. Like you set them up. Then they do it to you and you do it together and do counterpoint. It electrifies my brain. It was the saddest thing when my neurology fucked up and I couldn't play properly. The nervous connections to my fingers don't work.

CHAPTER 13

The Year of Paul Kelly

'I don't remember but it could be true. If so, my apologies to Philip.' – Singer–songwriter Paul Kelly

Young Philip loved music. While he wasn't allowed to listen to mainstream rock and roll in a household writhing with fears of hip-swivelling temptations like Elvis Presley, his mother bought him a $15 guitar. 'I've still got it. It was a German factory job, 3-ply. It's damaged; I now use it as a lap slide. I taught myself, worked it out. You could buy Christian hymn books with the very basic chords.' He breaks into a rendition of 'There is power, power, wonder-working power in the blood of the Lamb', from 1899.

'I listened to Segovia – I could get away with him at home. World Record Club [a UK mail-order firm selling LPs and reel-to-reel tapes] releases.' Philip was seven years old when he saw his first guitar. It belonged to a female country singer, name forgotten – though not the vision of her black-and-white leather skirt and cowboy boots. The lad was hooked in the second it took her to click open the case. 'It had all that crushed velvet inside,' he says, sounding like that enchanted little boy. 'When she took the guitar out, it made a *fywowying* noise. I was gone.'

The encounter took place in May 1960, on the night of Princess Margaret's wedding to 'commoner' and photographer Antony

Armstrong-Jones. It was the first royal ceremony to be televised in Australia, and Philip says our TV transmission was sped up so it could be viewed. All the same, there was no television set in the White household, and Philip himself has never owned one. As he grew into his teenaged years and managed to locate more contemporary music, Philip found solace in country rock from the US. 'I was up to my neck in anything like the Nitty Gritty Dirt Band with *Will The Circle Be Unbroken* and the Band with *Music From Big Pink*.'

Philip's first foray into live music was before leaving home, with friends who didn't even bother to have a band name, playing anonymously. 'First band, we played in the stables out the back of one of the pubs in Mt Barker. My father wasn't meant to know about it.' All up, Philip appeared in half-a-dozen local bands over a period of about a decade. 'I was heavily influenced by the Neil Young dirty sound. Marshall amps. Neil had just released his second album, *Everybody Knows This is Nowhere*.'

One hot day came a knock on the door of the house Philip was sharing on Fullarton Road. Nonplussed and wishing for a quieter life, he opened up to find 'a little Irish man' standing there with his acoustic guitar. 'No box,' noted Philip, rather sternly, as he is a stickler for instrument protection. 'He reminded me of Bob Dylan, and it turns out he really believed he was Dylan. I think he was impressed by my knowledge.'

Kelly, still standing at the door: 'I want to start a band.'

'So he came into my bedroom and we sat there and talked for a while and decided to have a go.'

Filmmaker Gus Howard was still part of the scene. He recalls an event that wasn't pinned down with any meaning until later. Gus and Philip had formed a firm friendship, begun when they were neighbours and their rock band 'seethed' in four rooms of a house 'famous for exuding more noise than had ever been heard in Stirling'. Philip fondly recalls: 'I slept with Gus Howard's vintage Rogers' drum kit, various guitars and a bright orange Marshall stack.'

Gus Howard was alongside during the growth of Philip's reputation as a guitarist and performer:

> Philip called me one day and I went and played with him and Peter with Paul Kelly in a house in North Adelaide. And I didn't really understand it at the time but that was an audition for Philip to work with Paul. We just went and jammed and it wasn't a thing we'd normally do. It was a bit off and Paul Kelly was standing at the corner looking at us like a bloody hawk. I felt quite awkward and thought: What the hell are we doing this for?

And so began Philip's tenure in The Debutantes. The line-up – at various stages – included drummer J.J. Hackett (Stars and Mondo Rock) and James Black (Rockwiz Orkestra, Men At Work, Mondo Rock).

Philip recalls the early days:

> I was writing songs with five chords and a Steely Dan feel. Jazzy things. I said, 'We'll have a jam, we'll get together. We can talk about this but I want to do some of my songs too, if we're going to share a band. Because it sounds like you want me to help you a lot with this.'
>
> We just did some of his songs; they were all pretty easy, just three chords like Johnny Cash. He couldn't do any of my songs. He'd come to every practice with five songs of his own. And there would be ten to twelve or thirteen of us trying to learn these new songs when we had a band practice; we never got to rehearse anything we'd already learned. There were too many people in the band, it was fucking nuts. He couldn't do any of my songs. And there were too many musicians. He was obsessed with just

> getting into the smack. And with Dylan's Rolling Thunder Revue. So he was wearing a scarf and all that stuff. He saw us all as his little soldiers. He really thought he was Dylan, he really thought he was the Prophet. And we had big rivalry.

Philip was beginning to see the potential around him. Andrew Zweck, 'a Lutheran law student from a farm in the Barossa', was acting as manager and had got the band a gig supporting John Mayall and the Blues Breakers. 'We were actually on the verge of pretty good success,' Philip says.

> The next day I said to Andrew, 'We've got to get serious here, we need to talk.' Andrew said, 'You're going to hate me; I'm going to live in London. I want to do the Rolling Stones.' Which he did. He became the boss of Wembley Stadium. Did Frank Sinatra. Toured everybody, the Stones and the Paul Simon concerts in Africa. Was production manager for Live Aid in 1985. Andrew still visits Adelaide from London. You'd be in his house and Eric Clapton would be walking out the door.

Zweck left but The Debutantes kept going. 'It was really tricky because the plan was to do half Paul's songs, half my songs,' Philip says.

> So we'd have the rehearsal and he would bring six new songs. And I'd say: 'Paul, we've got twelve or thirteen musicians, we've got a brass section, we've got pedal steel, we've got violins, we've got three guitars and girl singers. We've got to work out how to arrange the songs from last week before we learn more.' There was no chance of me getting my songs done.

It was clear Bob Dylan's Rolling Thunder Revue phase, which went for several years from 1975, had a major impact on Kelly. The sheer weight of the number of musicians made live sets hazardous to organise. Making matters worse, the notoriously headstrong Bob Dylan developed a habit of casually inviting others to join in with the band. According to Lou Kemp, a friend of Dylan's who eventually organised the tour, 'we would go out at night and run into people, and we'd just invite them to come with us. We started out with a relatively small group of musicians and support people. We ended up with a caravan.'

Obviously in an act of hero worship sparking imitation, Kelly would come into contact with a new crop of girl singers and he'd invite them along, ad hoc, without telling the others. 'So we'd play at the British or the Wellington or somewhere and there'd be three new girl singers Kelly had spotted in the audience the week before,' Philip says. 'It was crazy.' After about a year, Kelly rang. The conversation was immediately surreal and exceedingly embarrassing. Kelly sounded breathless, excited: 'I've got a new show, I'll leave some tickets for you at the door, Saturday night.'

> And I said, 'Paul, what do you mean you've got a new band? What happened to the other band?' He said, 'Oh, haven't I told you? I have a new band.' I asked him if he'd told any of the other musicians and he said, 'Nuh.'

It was a shock, but also a relief, according to Philip, whose opinion of Kelly was already on the way down. 'We all got sick of him going to sleep in his soup. On the nod at the table.' Philip claimed Kelly still denies the existence of The Debutantes, his first band. Almost forty years later that slight still hurts. Through his management, Kelly promptly responded to a set of questions relating to Philip's recollection.

Via email, Kelly said:

> Yes, I had a band called The Debutantes. Philip was in it. I have never denied its existence. I have talked about the band from time to time in interviews. I don't remember any song-writing arrangement though that could well have been the original intention.

On the veracity of Philip's version of that bizarre, band-breaking phone call, Kelly replied to this author's email question: 'I don't remember but it could be true. If so, my apologies to Philip. And as well as belated apologies, please send him my best.'

A clearer picture is revealed in legendary rock music writer Stuart Coupe's biography, *Paul Kelly: The Man, The Music, And The Life In Between* (Hachette 2020).

Nick Lainas, Philip's Adelaide University mate, is godfather to Paul's daughter Madeleine. Nick first met Paul in 1976, encountering what he describes as, 'a callow youth without much worldly experience at all'.

In *Paul Kelly*, Lainas talks of his first encounter with Paul:

> The first time I saw him, he was in a backyard with an acoustic guitar on his lap, and with this shock of incredible curly black hair. Paul was breaking free from all those conservative years of his Catholic upbringing. He was reading Henry Miller and writers like that. He wanted to disorganise his senses and extend his range of experiences, especially sexual ones. He had a level of determination even in those days. Paul was going to crash through. He wouldn't have lasted if he didn't have that – that iron will and focused vision. Music and songwriting became his total vision.

Coupe writes: 'It occurred to Paul that it was time to start a band – and one of the people he was going to start a band with was Adelaide musician and writer Philip White.' Philip, from an interview in the book:

> When we met I had been in a few bands that had had a modicum of success. I was a hillbilly preacher's kid, a full-on Bible-bashing jerk. It was all Bibles and shotguns for me. I must have seemed very exotic to Paul. I was pretty upfront. And Paul was a folk singer who hadn't really done very much. Both he and John thought they were Jack Kerouac. But I knew they weren't.

Coupe again:

> Up until then, Paul had been drifting around Adelaide playing solo as a Bob Dylan-inspired folkie at Ginger's coffee shop on Melbourne Street and other similar places around the city but this was his first foray into a rock'n'roll band. White and the others were much more experienced and able musicians. Paul was only 21 years old and, although he had learnt piano and trumpet as a child, he hadn't taken up the guitar until he was 18. There was much to learn.
>
> White feels that part of the erratic nature of The Debutantes was due to Paul's use of heroin, which he considered to be pretty serious when he lived in Adelaide. Whether Paul's dabbling with heroin was serious, or just outwardly so, White says that pretty early on he became alive to Paul's gritty determination and single focus. 'He was very easy to misunderstand because of his surly, quiet, almost receding nature but that belied a very heavy little ego and a determination which a lot of people didn't pick.'

Given Philip's claims that Kelly was attempting to erase the existence of The Debutantes, it is instructive that Coupe mentions not only the singer's drug abuse but also his deliberate moves to scrub evidence of his first two albums with the Dots: *Talk* and *Manila*. Kelly explained: 'When I gained control of my work in the late nineties, I simply chose not to make them available anymore. It wasn't the fault of the bands on those records. It was me.'

CHAPTER 14

Loving You is Easy But . . .

'Later at sunset I went for a walk and was looking at a very red Mars rising in the east and turned around and he was walking towards me down the dirt track and that was it.' – Maire Mannik

Philip's love life is laden with spice, mythology and controversy. It is no less volcanic and spellbinding than might be expected of a rambunctious pirate with the soul of a poet, a silver tongue and a whiff of gallant. If Philip has a 'type' – and that could be a parlour game full of folly – it is strong, independent and intelligent. One or two have been ardent feminists.

While it is futile and fatuous to gauge his lovers, several of his longer-term relationships have been with ambitious and clever women of the late twentieth century. Friends say he can be loud and opinionated, not afraid to talk himself up. When in full, funny, mesmerising, autodidactic flight, he is the very model of the cocksure alpha male. Yet . . . yet . . .

Friend Gus Howard: 'Philip has a strong feminine side. Loves women. He speaks of many strong women, usually on the older side.' In fact, Philip has often cared very deeply about the women in his life, to the extent that break-ups have sent him into a black, downward spiral for weeks on end. Artist George Aldridge: 'I've had to rescue him a few times. Drive halfway across the State to put him into a safe place.'

Wine, food and travel writer David Sly has a wonderful way of examining Philip – with a mixture of affection and realism.

> I've never seen Philip as predatory. He's always had extraordinary women around him. They are besotted with him until they're not besotted with him and suddenly there's a big trench between them, a trench that's filled with flaming oil [laughs].
>
> We've all seen the intensity with which Philip lived his life, it was full-on and a lot of women have been lured to the intellect, the pirate-poet – and the intensity's too much for everybody in the end. A lot going on with high passion. (David mimics a lover: 'Can't you spend more time with me?' And Philip: 'Nah, this is the stream I'm in.')
>
> Philip's very thoughtful. I see him as an Uncle Keith Richards sort of character, where there's more swagger and growl than there is bite. He knows that by taking hard lines and being blunt that people are going to want to have a go at him, so you need 'the armoury' to not get pulverised. You get challenged for what you write, you get wounded by that. But if you really believe in what you write, and you're prepared to defend it, you have to write what you believe to be the truth.

Whatever emotional ructions litter his past, there are signs Philip has mellowed. He jokes about having the testosterone sucked out of his manly body, replaced by estrogen, the primary female sex hormone. 'I am woman,' he jokes. The flailing, weaponised outbursts these days are few and far between, though Milton Wordley says he still cops a mouthful of the old Philip now and then.

One day, in early 2019, two women – one in her thirties, the other barely fifty – were up at his Yangarra vineyard cottage. Sun was shining on a still afternoon. Philip had been suffering what he called his 'morning sickness' caused by the aggressive treatment he was getting for a hostile, fast-spreading cancer that – at one stage – had threatened to kill him within six weeks. As one witness remarked: 'These women were all but on their knees, anointing his feet with restorative oils and soothing his brow with a cloth damp from his favourite perfume by Guerlain, cooing like mother doves.' What the witness didn't know until afterwards was that both were former lovers.

One was Monica Jansons, of Wirra Wirra wines, the other Annika Berlingieri, of Sellicks Hill Wines, and the daughter of Settlement Wines founder, Vincenzo 'Enzo' Berlingieri.

Both have long since happily re-partnered. They have been successful in the hospitality world and also reliable regulars in the volunteer crew quietly led by Milton, whose members have driven Philip several times and hundreds of kilometres a week to Flinders Medical Centre for chemo and assorted treatments, the chemist, the supermarket and the bottle shop. Without them all, Philip would be stranded, or financially crippled by taxi bills.

One of the most intimate, clear-eyed assessments of Philip comes from a woman who first encountered the mesmerising sage of the Exeter Hotel when she was sixteen, and who was never romantically involved with him. Tanya Bensimon is the daughter of Adelaide jeweller Albert 'No-Hoo-Haa' Bensimon, who was so fascinated by the offbeat cadences of Exeter regulars like Philip that he brought along Tanya and her brother Toby, for an 'education'. Now grown up and working in Melbourne, Tanya heard about the wine writer's diagnosis with rabid cancer. She wrote a touching letter that gives a feminine but neutral insight to a bloke's bloke who never married or had children.

Dear Philip,

I have no expectation for you to write back to me. I feel compelled to write and remind you of some of my favourite and not so favourable Philip moments.

I was very sad when I heard about your diagnosis and a few vivid memories of Philip moments came back to me. I met you at the Exeter Hotel and I was a student, you took so little interest in me, I felt like a fly and you were constantly trying to swish me away. But your conversations, your controversial points of view, your strength of character, not only made you fascinating it made every encounter one that was rich with discussion. You became my literary hero. Even when you were pissed you were more eloquent than when most people are sober and I just hung around to learn from you. Eventually you and I became friends and I don't think it was merely because of your budding friendship with Dad because you are no bullshit. If you hadn't liked me you would have found a clever strategy to avoid me.

It's a little nerve-wracking writing to someone like you, I am sure I have made numerous grammatical errors already and no doubt they are bugging the shit out of you.

My second memory is of one of my first times at T-Chow, I was sitting next to you and you said, 'Tanya taste this wine it's beautiful and it's not expensive, it's made by some mates of mine and I rate it highly.' I naïvely broke the biggest wine sin of the wine world and took a sip from YOUR glass . . . You yelled, 'Great, now I have your fucking perfume in my glass,' then you hesitated for a moment and proceeded to name every ingredient in my perfume and finally the brand.

Once you invited Dad and I up to your house when you were living above the Botanical and for the first time you declared that you considered me to be a good friend. I was so elated because

I had always been filled with such admiration for you but up until that point I felt like a tick trying to get under your skin. It wouldn't have deterred me from persisting.

Another beautiful memory is of your spectacular handwritten notebooks with illustrations. The first time you showed them to me I realised that my suspicions about you were correct and that you were in fact a creative genius – but more than that I realised you were a sabra. Prickly on the exterior; warm, sweet and soft on the inside. The top 100 was fun, I remember sharing some sneaky leftovers with you. I also learnt that brushing your teeth prior to a monumental task like that is not the way to go and that plaque actually serves to protect your teeth. I still brushed mine before we polished off some of the best leftovers!

I realise that you have an abundance of friends and due to the tyranny of distance, not just my move to Melbourne but also yours to the country, we have not maintained regular contact. I just want you to be aware of the impact you have had on me since I was 16 years old. Philip, you have inspired me, infuriated me when you had your grumpy moments, argued so beautifully that you managed to tilt the prism of life and let me look at issues from a different perspective. I consider myself to be one of the lucky ones who was allowed to enjoy the soft warm sweet interior of the sabra that you are. For this I am grateful.

I am finding the news about your health very hard to accept and I want you to know that I love and admire you.

Tanya x

PS: Please don't let any spelling or grammatical errors distract from the sentiment in this message, there are very few wordsmiths who will ever measure up to you and I wouldn't even try.

In the early seventies, Maire Mannik, 'an Estonian intellectual', was Philip's first serious girlfriend. She had already started the Women's Liberation Movement in Adelaide, along with writer Anne Summers and lauded chef Cath Kerry, who also had a feisty and not altogether happy relationship with the Kanmantoo Kid. 'Actually that says something decent about him,' Maire says. 'For such an alpha male to accept all the lecturing and rules was surprising.' Maire walks her talk, saying she was: first woman in SA to get a mortgage without a male guarantor; first female IT manager in the State public service; and first woman in Australia to get a David Jones credit card without revealing her marital status.

She met Philip at a mutual friend's house in Renown Park one night in June 1973.

> We went off somewhere in his big Valiant and when I saw seven Bibles on the back shelf I went total atheist outrage. He played along and we argued the length of the trip. Of course it was his father's car. First impressions: loud, boorish, very good at arguing. He had his twenty-first birthday party and I went to that.
>
> His parents were off doing bigotry in the US so it was in their house and the Kanmantoo Institute. He invited me to come back on the Labour Day weekend. We spent the Saturday with Peter Wright on acid. I had only taken it once before the previous year and it was a combination of a perfect day with two extraordinary people, the hills still green. Later at sunset I went for a walk and was looking at a very red Mars rising in the east and turned around and he was walking towards me down the dirt track and that was it. The following week he wrote me a letter about it all and I went back the next weekend, which was when it started.

Pulled together by a love of language and music, they were both regulars at Mother's import record shop in Coromandel Place before actually meeting. Maire was into Dylan, the Beatles and the blues. Country and western, on the other hand, was for yokels and rednecks.

> Philip introduced me to all of that. Albums of truck-driving songs, Little Feat, The Dillards, unknowns such as Jackson Browne, Commander Cody, Dan Hicks, all the alternative stuff from California. And I still listen to them. When my iPod shuffle plays certain tracks, it is a hot Friday evening again in 1973 and I am waiting for him in front of the library on North Terrace.
>
> I also had a head full of mathematics and on our first date at the Eagle on the Hill I derived Euler's formula, which is the most beautiful thing in the universe, in fine ink pen on the menu.

The two started working together as a consequence of Maire's early stand against tobacco, which happens to be one of Philip's sources of enjoyment.

> After two years as a programmer at the government's Automatic Data Processing Centre all hell broke loose because I asked to be moved from a desk in front of two chain smokers. When I returned from unpaid leave, I was sent to the Mines Department in its rundown old building on the corner of Rundle and Pulteney. I was the IT Manager at the Department of Mines. In 1975 he was a Field Assistant in the Information Branch, which dealt with providing information to the public. As soon as he finally got the job at Mines – just after I had moved to Stirling and he had moved in – he immediately bought an expensive Gibson guitar, and then another, and then an amplifier and his entire salary went on paying off the loans. Some of the private conversations were fascinating.
>
> My reading is wide and various and he would have heard all about quantum physics and the Eighteenth Dynasty and the Bloomsbury group. You name a social ill and I knew it was wrong long before it became fact. I went through the sixties as

> an anti-smoker. Imagine. My first house in 1968 had a big No Smoking sign on the door. Unheard of. I left that out of our first meeting. He was the only smoker in the room. But he gave up and didn't smoke except for the odd cigar outside while we were together. Then he started again. When I met him it was mainly Jack Daniels and Jim Beam. I started him on fine wines. As one of the Henschke [wine dynasty] sons said, I have a lot to answer for.

Clearly Philip was anything but dull as a boyfriend. The rewards were great but so was the price. 'We were all so young then and put up with a lot of shit we would not have done later,' Maire says.

> Also we were inventing the rules as we went along. Just out of the seventies and feminism was still so new. He definitely wanted to be the centre of attention, which was made much worse after a few drinks. Also he would become verbally belligerent often because he misunderstood something. He used to chat women up in front of me. Not exactly: 'How about a root, darl?' but more: 'Let me know you think I'm wonderful.'

Maire recalls a train trip to Melbourne and the amusement brought by a trip to Georges glamorous department store. 'Philip was very fit then and dressed in cowboy denim. I swear as we walked in those revolving doors there was a loud hiss as every gay salesman had a loud intake of breath. We were besieged by helpful assistants.'

Journalist Colin James: 'Women find him incredibly attractive.' On a more gender-neutral note, Colin, who is very fond of Philip, adds:

> There is a dark side. You can sense it, feel it. It's a brooding within him. But that's what comes from a man of his intellect. People as clever as him tend to look at the world very analytically and get burdened by that. Look at Stephen Fry, for instance.

I've got a friend that sends me wine in a taxi
Some people say he drinks too much so what
They're only judging wine by the label
And not the thirst to match his big big heart

From '*Wine in a Taxi*', one of singer–songwriter Tubby Justice's songs to Philip

Tubby Justice now resides in Melbourne, and has a daughter, Billie, an artist who lives in Adelaide and whose father is Mark Thomson. Here, she tells the story of her long-standing friendship with Philip.

I had moved from Melbourne to Brisbane. I was seventeen and looking for a penfriend. That's when Mark Ulbrich, my old friend from Adelaide University, said I've got the perfect person for you. His name is Philip White and he lives in Adelaide. He was maybe twenty-two or three, which seems a lot older.

I had no intentions of ever coming to Adelaide. I wrote Philip a letter and he wrote back. He was an exceptionally good letter writer. I don't spend much time on them because I write very quickly. Whereas Philip had this incredible hand, this beautiful handwriting. He used the pens the architects used. And he'd put little drawings in and various things. Always beautiful paper. He always had 'God Speed' written on the back of the envelope.

I was reading a Richard Brautigan book. There must have been something in the book – could have been *Trout Fishing In America* – that mentioned waterfalls. So I offered to sell Philip a waterfall. That's how come we started writing. Over the years, intermittently. Sometimes we'd stop and we'd be busy with our lives.

When I finally met Philip, he was nothing like I thought he'd be. Cos I thought: This bloke is a cowboy, probably . . . and an exceptional writer. Semi-careful and neat the way he wrote. Incredibly knowledgeable. He introduced me to South Australia. History. Sold me on Adelaide, though not deliberately. I came to Adelaide to see Kurt Vonnegut Jnr at Writer's Week; I'd already bought my ticket. Then he cancelled because they wouldn't let his partner come because they weren't formally married. So Kurt said, I'm sorry, but I'm not coming. Flying then cost a fortune so I thought I'd go to Adelaide anyway.

Having that religious education was very telling in terms of his knowledge. He never said a bad word about his parents, ever. He'd tell me hilarious – sometimes disturbing – stories about them. But never would he say they were bad people, or I was hard done by. The vomiting duck fat story – his dad drank all of the duck fat out of the pan and projectile-vomited it out again. At the time, when you're talking and listening and exchanging stories and laughter, you don't think, I'd better remember all this. Like that John Cale song: 'The best of times with the thoughtless kind.'

Philip is really my brother, he feels like my brother. I never knew the day that I wrote that first letter that this would be the person that I would love till the day I die.

You never know where you're going to find these people. And there are only a few in your life. I got a great education from Philip. So he would send me these wonderful music compilation tapes and magazines and suggest books. I was just a straight sort of Motown soul girl when we met, and jazz. If he finds it interesting, he will tell you. I was seventeen. I wasn't old enough to even drink.

Philip lived in one of the squares in town and I lived in Parkside. I can't remember exactly what happened, but I'd thought, I'll just go down and get the wine for a dinner party or whatever was going on. The pubs weren't open and I don't drive. This was around 1994 or 1995. I phoned Philip and asked, 'Have you got any wine, I'm desperate.' He said, 'Sure.' I said, 'Throw it in a cab and I'll pay for it at my end.' I just wanted a small amount but he sent me a boxful. I woke up the next day and started running round the house and started singing that song 'Wine in a Taxi'. I've got a friend that sends me wine in a taxi. That was actually pretty easy, that song.

We never formally went out, Philip and I – ever. He's one of the people in my life who hold up the sky. He's solid, a true authentic person and hardly an aggressive bone in his body. He is a big gentle man. He was an intelligent person and he'd say stuff that would aggravate the shit out of somebody and they knew they couldn't win so they would hit him. He's like a tomcat; he blows himself up and his whole stance changes.

A lot of people are fascinated by Philip, and if he leaves the relationship they get resentful. How dare you not be interested in our friendship any more? I arrived in Adelaide around 1978 or 1979. Don Dunstan was still here. This was certainly a huge village that I could live in. I met a lot of friends. I don't think I could have done things with music if I had stayed in Melbourne. I loved Rundle Street; I started cooking in restaurants. I knew Mr Randall's. They used to sell ginger beer by the glass. Charlick's was still a grain store. The original Ruby's Cafe. I thought, This is my town. I started cooking with Wally Selis, at Lark and Tina's. Philip Searle and Barry Ross.

I won a talent contest at Lark and Tina's – with Phil Colson, a great guitarist. Now lives in Sydney. He's Sia's dad, she's now an international music star. That's what you could do in Adelaide. You could just know people. Whereas with Melbourne it was pockets, little precincts all over the place. We had a lot of local success. And in Melbourne too. Steve Matters was my musical partner; he was fantastic. I left Adelaide ten years ago.

The irony is that Philip worked at the Department of Energy and Mines, which is where Mark Ulbrich's dad was, Brendan

Thomson. And Philip knew Brendan before any of us had ever met. My father's a cook, and it was the last thing I was going to do, become a cook. But I loved it. I stopped full-time cooking when I went back to Melbourne. I thought Philip was quintessentially South Australian, even though he was born in Victoria. I love it because he acts like a twelve-year-old boy when I say: 'How are you, Philip?' and he replies, 'Very well thank you, Tubby.'

Wine in a Taxi

I've got a friend that sends me wine in a taxi
Some people say he drinks too much so what
They're only judging wine by the label
And not the thirst to match his big big heart.
He used to say, oh darling Tubby you'll be fine this time
Just look around you know you'll find me here
I'm always near no need to cry alone.
He used to write and call me whispy mystery
But that was long before we knew
That time can play a trick with history
Sing us the same song second verse.

And now he says, oh darling Tubby you'll be fine tonight
Just look for me I'll be an inch away oh you can stay
No need to be alone.
I love the man who sends me wine in a taxi
You know he's got a great big thirsty heart
I read between the lines in the letters
Oh Mr White there etched upon my heart.

Baby and eldest child Philip Christopher, born at Warragul Hospital, Victoria, with his mother, Sylvia May White (nee Seymour). His father, Pastor Jimmy White, is holding the pram. (The woman at top left is unknown, possibly the nanny.)

Philip on the shoulders of his paternal grandfather Andrew James White. 'I was his first grandchild, and his favourite,' says Philip. 'And I was the only one who understood how crook he was with PTSD after serving in the trenches of WWI.'

The White family in the backyard at Kanmantoo in 1968.
Back, left to right: Sylvia White and Philip. Paul, Stephen and Andrew are in the middle; Mark and Helen at front.

Falconers: Three White brothers and a Ford Falcon circa 1972. From left: Stephen, Paul and Andrew (who died in a car accident). 'Mum and Dad were preaching in the US, so we used his car. That car had really good tyres to hold the road, and three-on-the-tree. The boys were visiting me at Wayside Cottage in Stirling, where I lived with teacher Helen Becze and her husband Tony, who was then studying anthropology at Flinders Uni.'

Philip in a 1969 photograph from the Mt Barker High School magazine *Orbit*, which he edited.

Centre, front: Ms Ieva Kains, Philip's favourite teacher at Mt Barker High. Philip, aged 17, is standing on the left. Ieva, who taught English, also introduced the class to a diverse range of music, from Beethoven to Dylan.

Philip, captured while helping out on a yacht built by Jean-Pierre Kerry, younger brother of legendary Adelaide chef Cath Kerry.

If Philip looks angry, it is because he was – over anti-Semitic graffiti on the fence of his abode at Little Archer Street, North Adelaide.

Philip performing Everly Brothers songs at Medindie in 1978.

A documentary film crew that also worked with Premier Don Dunstan. This still is from a 1981 government information film about a Whitlam-era initiative, The Parks Community Centre. Left to right: Mario Andreacchio (a successful movie director), Philip, director Gus Howard (*Blue Heelers*), Alfonso (surname unknown), Leak Cocks, Suresh Ayyar.
Gus: 'I either shot, or shot and produced, and Philip was my assistant, but we worked as a team in the same spirit as we played music. There was a plan and a lot of improvisation, and we kept just a little ahead of everyone around us.'

A study in ceramic: Philip after a big night on sherry (Mildara's Chestnut Teal) at a mate's home in the Hills.

Philip, in Musketeer mode, with then girlfriend Monica Jansons in the early 90s.

A 1982 cover of the short-lived arts magazine *Ash*. Left to right: Philip, Nick Lainas and editor John Kingsmill. The then-unknown musician Paul Kelly was in charge of layout.

A cherished weekly lunch at T-Chow in Adelaide's Chinatown began in 1989 and still runs. It is used by Philip as an excuse for a bit of wine tasting among like-minded friends.

Max Schubert, who was forced to work his Grange magic in secret, under the noses of his ultra-conservative bosses at Penfolds.

Love and hate: This sums up Philip's relationship with influential Barossa winemaker the late Peter Lehmann, drinking from his just-won Stoddart Trophy. (Photo Milton Wordley)

Former friends Philip and Wolf Blass, with Wolf's right-hand man John Glaetzer in the background. Mateship has not survived the full journey for wine writer and winemaker.

Prime Minister John Howard with Philip at the opening of the O'Leary-Walker winery at Watervale in the Clare Valley in 2010. Winemaker David O'Leary's brother Tony was longtime press secretary to the PM.

Legends celebrating Dr Ray Beckwith's 100th birthday (left to right): Don Ditter, Penfolds winemaker; Ray Beckwith, AM, a wine chemist who employed Max Schubert, father of Grange; Philip; and winemaker John Bird, who was with Penfolds for almost all Grange vintages. (Photo Richard Humphrys)

Pastor Jimmy White's funeral, August 2013, after the burial, in Callington Hall.
Left to right: Stephen, Paul, Helen, Sylvia, Philip and Mark. 'Mum said at the time she would wait until Christmas to die,' Philip says. 'And when we all got together again, just before the 25 December in 2013, she went.'

Philip, peering down on the coffin containing his father, Pastor Jimmy White.
'I hated him, he was a bully.' (Photo Mick Wordley)

Philip with one of his great friends, late restaurateur Tony Bilson. 'He ran a string of great restaurants in Melbourne and Sydney,' Philip says. 'Started out cooking chops in a pub, and he's the godfather of it all really, contemporary Australian cuisine.'

'I wasn't intending to look like a rabbi – it just happened that way.'

Philip, with his gold medal from the American Independent Publishers, New York Book Show, 2014, for his contribution to photographer Milton Wordley's acclaimed coffee-table book, ***A Year in the Life of Grange.***

Wine writ large: The 2013 launch of Milton Wordley's ***A Year in the Life of Grange***.
Left to right: Penfolds chief winemaker Peter Gago, designer John Nowland, Milton Wordley and Philip.

70th birthday celebrations at the Old Lion Hotel, for mutual friend, Dr Bob de Bellevue, dermatologist to the stars, based in New Orleans. Left to right: Philip, then Premier Jay Weatherill, Kelly Menhennett playing guitar, Anna Bouras.

'The look': No words required when Philip thought you were a fool, as Anne-Marie Shin is discovering.

The late Bob McLean, who made his mark as an ambassador for the wine industry and could mix in the most exalted circles without special introduction, c. 1988. Seen behind is Philip's beloved powder-blue 1977 Valiant V8, an ex-police pursuit car nicknamed Shiva.

'Nadine', another ex-lover, says of Philip:

> He's a real mixture of his mum and his dad. He had this macho image, which was protecting a very soft centre. That's the mum part of him. He's a very vulnerable person and I think that's what I loved about him. That's what women fall for. The first time I met his parents, I'll never forget the look on his mother's face. She emanated unconditional love. So pleased to see Philip. She just had this loving, loving, loving face. And she walked up to him and put her hands on his face, it was just beautiful. I can remember thinking: That's where Philip gets that side. He's an extraordinarily loving person. Here was this person who looked like a bit of a bogan, but with a massive brain; and a fascinating range of stuff to talk about.
>
> We did have some fabulous times together. So much fun. We used to go on road trips. I remember driving to Sydney for [leading chef] Tony Bilson's wedding to Amanda. Philip would always pack, to go on a road trip, however long or short. He'd choose really carefully a selection of music and books and he would read to me while I drove.
>
> It was just a beautiful thing. He used to read fabulous stuff to me – not just when I was driving. He had such eclectic tastes in literature and music and he'd read things out to me from the *Spectator* and the *New Scientist* that I would never have known about or found by myself and so I loved that. We got invited to a lot of things. We were living a high-octane social life. Invited to all the big wine events and gourmet weekends and goodness knows what.

In the years spent with Philip, she noticed he rarely visited his parents. When he did – and she always accompanied him – Philip didn't tell them he was coming, even one Christmas Day. 'That was typical of Philip, he would never commit to anything in case he decided against it at the last minute or got a better offer. And that goes for everything.'

Except for one episode later in Philip's life, the hot topic of babies was pretty much out of bounds. Philip:

> I was that terrified of my father, that I would be like him. I quite deliberately never had children. I couldn't trust myself not to lose it. And now when I look back, I think I probably would have been a lot better than him. Sometimes I regret it but that's a pretty big decision to make when you're nineteen.

CHAPTER 15
Backs to the Blast

'Philip is very much of a period when SA was in the ascendancy . . . such a brilliantly perverse personality throughout all of that.' – Christian Kerr

Journalist Christian Kerr remembers Adelaide when it had rather more confidence in its place on the national stage:

> Philip is very much of a period when SA was in the ascendancy. Which is why he became such a national figure. There was that explosion of the Australian wine industry in the eighties. We're talking about a time when people were drawn to SA, or at least stopped by to see what was happening. Philip was such a brilliantly perverse personality throughout all of that.
>
> I remember this rather wild, big-drinking, big-talking, often-talking-himself-up, bursting-with-words, larger-than-life wine writer. There's so much horrible wankery about wine writing but he never seemed to have that. He seemed to have so much inspiration, and come from so many different angles, that when you actually met the man you could see he was so much like his writing. He was just such a presence and you were a little bit scared and intimidated but at the same time this was a challenge.
>
> So you would get into a conversation at the Exeter. He was there a lot. It was one of the things I think Dunstan did successfully for both the people he attracted and those of the same calibre around him; he really stressed the cultural aspects

of SA in the seventies. He made SA so much of a cultural powerhouse, so much of a cultural centre, that it covered up our relative economic decline during that period. I think that influence spilled over into the eighties and then suddenly all the money had really gone and so much more money was available if you wanted to run off to Sydney, in particular. Adelaide was left completely bereft. We've lost so much ground to places like Margaret River and Tasmania. The restaurant scene in Adelaide has picked up, but there was a fallow period.

In the eighties it wasn't only the young ones who left Adelaide. You had the author and historian Geoffrey Dutton leaving. Again you've got to put Philip down as a central part of that exodus. Even on a subcultural level, at one stage in the early eighties you had the Mod revivalists hanging out at the Aurora Hotel in Hindmarsh Square. But then you'd go to places like the Exeter and meet any group from the bohemians to the skinheads or whatever. A brief period with so many different groups. The food and wine in the background was spectacular and really influencing us.

The crucial thing is SA just ran out of money. The party came to an end. But I still think of SA as the wine capital, it's still strong. Art, food and wine has been able to fill the gap left behind by the end of manufacturing – not in the way of replacing the jobs or the income, but from the point of view of making the place matter.

I've been away from Adelaide for twenty-odd years but the small bar culture does seem to have taken root, a food and wine culture does seem to be coming back to SA. You don't have people singing the praises of SA in a very individual style (like Philip's) these days. Culture does not substitute for a strong economic base. But culture is power. SA mightn't have a brilliant economy, but culture can make it nationally significant and improve the quality of life within.

Back in the mid-seventies, young people were moving to Adelaide, rather than moving out. Harry Bardwell was part of the trend. 'In 1977 I moved from Perth to Adelaide', he wrote.

> I thought Don Dunstan's South Australia with the SAFC was the happening place for film in Australia. I created my own production company Composite Films and began making corporate documentaries for the SAFC with the likes of Ron Saunders, Justin Milne, Andrew Prowse, Gus Howard and Geoff Simpson.

Bardwell's faith in Adelaide was to prove pivotal for the fortunes of Philip and Gus Howard via a groundbreaking documentary, *Backs to the Blast*, released in 1980. Gus was cinematographer, Philip was the publicist providing material gathered while he was working for the Mines Department and had, unwittingly, handled materials from Maralinga. The ghost of Maralinga would come to haunt Philip, more than forty years after his stint as Core Library Controller cataloguing core samples from mines across the State.

At one point, tensions in the Mines Department building rose because of suspicions about what the British Defence Force had *not* told them about some of the samples. The fear escalated when Philip received a strange call from a British Major speaking from Lucas Heights in NSW, home of Australia's first nuclear reactor. Not only was the call unexpected, it was also unexplained. The Major had ordered Philip to ship Maralinga plutonium samples to him at Lucas Heights ASAP, or 'you'll be in really dead trouble'. Thoughts racing, Philip reminded himself Lucas Heights was a civilian – not military – installation. He asked his boss why a British army officer was hassling him. 'It was really scary,' Philip says.

Backs to the Blast blew the lid off the secrecy that had hitherto shrouded the British-inspired scandal of Maralinga in the desert west of Port Augusta. This was the trial site for British nuclear tests in the later 1950s and 1960s. 'The whole thing had been out of sight and out of mind,' Bardwell said. 'A cover-up that was coming to light.' The dudes of Rundle Street were buzzing.

Bardwell might never have made the film (budget below $50,000) had it not been for chance conversations with Michael 'Zippy' Zerman about stories he wrote for *Digger* magazine while living in Sydney. Zerman had spoken to veteran soldiers who had been damaged at Maralinga, including one who developed agoraphobia.

'I had never heard of Maralinga until then,' says Zerman, who came back from Sydney to see what was happening in SA and to run the SA Media Resource Centre. Bardwell, who had also been in the dark, confesses:

> It took me years to realise Zippy's seminal role in the film. I started interviewing the veterans. Many were ill. They told me eye-opening stories of working without safety gear in the desert, having to go into radioactive hotspots, flying through plumes after the bombs had exploded. Cinesound had newsreels of men turning their backs to the atomic blasts, and in Canberra I found footage of Jeremy Long rounding up nomadic Aborigines to make way for the tests.

Later, the film was screened for the Yalata mob, who had been forcibly removed from their traditional homeland to a barren stretch of the Nullarbor Plain. In the audience was Jack Davis, one of the traditional owners of the Maralinga test site. When it came to the scene showing the bomb detonated, Jack began to shake uncontrollably. Bardwell kept pressing ahead, despite some negative reaction. 'Everyone began getting edgy,' he recalls.

> It was announced that anti-nuclear activists were now identified as ASIO's number one most subversive citizens. Was it paranoia or had my phone started clicking mysteriously. Notes disappeared from my car, had I left them somewhere? By the time we had finished the film, nuclear vets were in the news. It was a hot story.
>
> Eventually, the British Government agreed to fund two clean-ups of the test site, in particular identifying and collecting plutonium fragments left from the tests at Maralinga. Overall, I understand the clean-ups cost the Brits in excess of 100 million dollars. The Maralinga people had their land returned to them in 1985 and were later compensated $13.5 million dollars for their mistreatment. Subsequently there have been several attempts by nuclear veterans to hold a class action for compensation for their treatment but they have not been successful. Many have already died.

CHAPTER 16

Blood on the Typewriter

'From 1974 to 1981, these were my almost accidental years of good training.' – Philip White

The road to swirling wine in a glass and examining its beauty or beastliness was long and winding for Philip. He is the first to point out that when he left home, 'I was smoking dope, dropping acid and drinking Bourbon.'

His career can be difficult to follow, because it was not in his nature to seek the security of a cadetship at the successful newspapers of the time, the *Advertiser* or the *News*. Philip went where the wind blew him.

First, in 1978, came the *Adelaide Preview*, precursor to the *Adelaide Review*. Mainly the arts and rock and roll, under stewardship of Terry Plane. Then followed a stint editing the Adelaide-based national publication *Winestate*, in 1981. By 1982, Philip was in Sydney, editing the *Wine & Spirit Buying Guide*, started by Len Evans, an English-born Australian promoter, maker, judge, taster and teacher of wine. Evans, according to *The Oxford Companion to Wine*, 'did more to advance the cause of wine in Australia than any other individual'. Next came the *National Times*, with Philip creating a stir because his arrival prompted the departure of James Halliday. Then the *Advertiser*, which came after a typical exchange with then editor Piers Akerman. Akerman: 'Why aren't you working for me?' Philip: 'Because you've never asked.' In later years, Philip's work has regularly appeared in online paper *InDaily*.

The seventies and eighties suited, as contemporaries kicked out the jams of the postwar era. Philip was a member of Don Dunstan's film crew in the mid-seventies. 'Don would come in hungover, unshaven and dishevelled, and grumpy as all hell and Kevin Crease [later a TV newsreader] would clean him up, put him in a suit and tie,' Philip says.

> But he was a beauty, because he needed only three takes at the most to get it right. Don could be demanding and bossy – he had to be. But if you did the right thing, he'd never forget you. His wife, Adele Koh, ran the office like a sea captain. You couldn't get into his joint unless she let you.

Dunstan had made his name in the 1960s. As Attorney-General he brought SA into line with the rest of the Commonwealth by allowing hotel bars to stay open until 10 pm. Philip believes Dunstan's legacy may be under-appreciated these days. 'He was more significant than we think,' he says, using the example of the battle to bring al fresco to Adelaide, which had the 'widest unused footpaths in the world'.

The teenaged Philip – like so many of his baby boomer generation – was spoiled for choice. It was the era of the cry: 'I had the offer of three different jobs in the same morning!' Adelaide regarded itself as the third city, behind Sydney and Melbourne. None of this 'backwater' rubbish. The Thomas Playford years had boosted industry and growth. Don Dunstan's touch-of-arts class dragged South Australia out of the Age of Wowserism and was so socially progressive that he turned heads in Sydney and Melbourne. For all that, the months around Philip's thirtieth birthday were inauspicious, partly because he had just finished a job and had a tickle in his pocket. 'I had money,' he remembers.

> But I also was 200 yards from the Havelock Hotel. I'd get up in the morning, go down the pub and just sit there and drink and weep, basically. It was getting close to Christmas and my friends were getting worried about me. John Kingsmill – who I had worked with before on the *Adelaide Review* – rang and said, 'I've got a job for you.' I remember saying, 'I don't want a job.' He said, 'No, no. You can keep drinking. This wine magazine I do the layout for needs an editor. You understand colour production and editing, so let's do it. We can work together and have fun.' So, I ended up editor of *Winestate* magazine.

These days it is described as Australia's most respected and oldest wine magazine, with an international circulation of 350,000.

Difficult to imagine now, but Philip was raw back in 1981. Publisher Peter Simic asked him if he'd ever been to a proper wine tasting. 'Not really,' replied Philip. 'I just like drinking it. Why?' The answer was Seppelts, which had its head office at the German Club in Pirie Street and had just won the Jimmy Watson trophy. The brief was simply 'to take notes and write down what you think of the wines'. And that's what was delivered – those 'live-in-the-moment' notes in quite clear handwriting, with none of the conventional structure. 'They appeared in the next issue of the magazine, untouched, and I got the job.'

The hillbilly bohemian magic-mushroom muncher introduced himself to his three members of staff. And the accountant. 'I was making a good name for myself,' Philip says. 'I had men like

Max Lake and serious people in Sydney saying, "Hey what's this dude doing?" I changed the look of the magazine and the way it worked.'

By 2019, *Winestate* was celebrating forty-one years recording the history of Australian wine. Such a pedigree was unthinkable to the young Simic in 1978. And he had a problem: who was to fill his shoes when he left – very soon – for the United States to set up a new wine magazine over there? A young, brash bloke 'who had been working for IBM and a rock music publication' was offered the job of editor in 1981. 'We hired Philip because he was cheap and available quickly,' Simic recalls. 'Our editor at the time was pissed off that he didn't get the USA opportunity and quit.'

Even then, there was no strong evidence the new executive knew anything much about wine. 'He'd just swan around, doing lunches and mixing with winemakers,' Simic says. 'Then the deadlines would catch up with him – and he would work endless hours – put in long nights on end. He used to call those sessions "blood on the typewriter".'

> When Peter Simic gave me that job at *Winestate*, I couldn't believe my luck. Not because I had all that wine, but because I had access to these great men, leaders in the industry. David Wynn. Max Schubert. Wolf Blass. Jack Kilgore. All these old men who'd made wine before the War as well as after it. I had the best education. For palate. Understanding the culture. Free education. Passion. Being paid to learn. It's water usage. It's international trade. It's biochemistry. It's about different rocks under the soil. It's the most fascinating field. It's not writing about milk. It's about public intoxication. And about all the things I'm interested in and can weave together in wine writing. I've had great fun being able to draw on all those great things, which no other wine writers do.

Simic, again:

> Philip at his best was recognised as the best wine writer in Australia. However, there were times of the possible drug-crazed meanderings of a lunatic. We never really gelled. He tolerated me because I was not your down-on-everything style with him. He never quite worked me out . . . I wasn't a journo type but then we were creating new things back then. He is a real character.

When Simic returned from the US, he discovered his strong-willed, fledgling editor had flown the coop, the office was in a degree of turmoil, and his *Winestate* operation was in need of prompt regenerative attention. Philip recalls the opportunity that came along, one too hard to pass up.

> My dear friend, Peter Lehmann, and I were at the big knees-up at the Vintage Festival in the Barossa. It would have been 1982. He told me he wanted me to meet an important man. It was John David, who had just bought the *Wine and Spirit Guide*, my rival magazine, which I was envious of because it was in Sydney, and had a bigger budget. It had four times the readership of *Winestate*.
>
> He could see a new wine wave coming – boutique wineries. He already knew how to distribute to supermarkets through his Black and Gold company, and he knew how to do liquor. So he set up a company called Australian Liquor Market and when I got to Sydney I discovered my role was to fudge the tastings so he could control all those new brands and products. I sat him down and told him: 'I don't have to fudge anything because you own the magazine. All I need to do is get proper judges to do these tastings and I'll let you know the results before we publish so you can ring the wineries and arrange the deal that you want.' The first year I was there, they turned over a billion dollars in groceries and liquor.

In an unfortunate turn of events two years later, Philip discovered he had a new boss.

> I went in one day and the company secretary said: 'You've got a new owner, Larry Pickering.' I said: 'What do you mean? You were going to sell it to me if you were going to sell it. I've built this magazine up and it's now really rocking and you've given it to Pickering.'

Philip had been thinking positively – he had a flat in Elizabeth Bay, and Sydney was the place to be. Fondly, on drinkster.com, Philip outlined the good times. Many of those memories were of Peter Doyle's Watson's Bay restaurant on the Harbour, 'where the Bob Hawke Cabinet made lunchtime deals, drank buckets of Pike's Clare Riesling and ate Australia's most expensive fish'n'chips.

'I watched it', Philip wrote.

> I lived in the convicts' quarters in Peter's backyard in his old South Head harbourmaster's house, complete with shackle rings in the stone at my bed head. The only rent he'd accept was advice with the wine list and the disposal of the pallets of empties that came out the tail of every mad lunch. He bought a glass grinder.
>
> Hawkie, of course, was teetotal. He stayed away. But Peter would climb on his favourite wee tender in the mornings after the fish market and putter across the harbour with the right bait and tack to pick the PM up and take him to where he knew he would catch a fish or two in the quiet.
>
> I'd be nose down editing *Wine & Spirit* across the harbour and Doyle would be on the phone at noon. 'Front table. Everyone's in. Got you a chair.' Water taxi. Madness. We enjoyed a different level of lobbying.

The news about the Pickering takeover of his baby came as a shock. Not least because the next edition had a radically different cover and page layout. 'It was shit.' A popular political cartoonist, Pickering won four successive Walkley Awards between 1971 and 1974. But towards the end of his life he went bankrupt and was variously accused of being a conman, scumbag racist and misogynist whose depictions of then Prime Minister Julia Gillard were condemned as vile. According to Philip, Pickering told him, 'I don't like you, you're a wine snob.'

> At that stage, James Halliday had been running the biggest wine column in Australia, in the *National Times*, the Fairfax weekly. It was the best investigative paper in Australia, ever. Walkley Award after Walkley Award. Wendy Bacon, Brian Toohey. I knew these people, just from hanging out in Sydney. It was big time for a little Kanmantoo boy. Jefferson Penberthy became editor of the *National Times* after Brian Toohey and he fired James Halliday and gave me the job of wine writer in 1984.
>
> It was a great promotion for me because they also needed a mining writer in Adelaide. I had a mining background, working in the mines at Kanmantoo as a kid and in the Mines Department. Roxby Downs was going. So I opened a Fairfax bureau in a distribution warehouse in Waymouth Street, just down from the *'Tiser*. I was covering Adelaide news and elections and stuff. Contributing to Clancy, which was the gossip page. It was exciting; I had lots of opportunities.

By 1986, the *National Times* had closed, and Philip found a home back in Adelaide at the *'Tiser*, then edited by Piers Akerman.

Which brings us to the geology of the McLaren Vale wine region map, the collective work of three geologists – Jeffrey Olliver, William Fairburn and Wolfgang Preiss – and Philip.

> Things like that gave me a fair bit of kudos not just here but internationally as somebody who's actually done something

> about making the theory of terroir more scientific. Because my map is a scientific document. I love science.

The map perfectly fits Philip's long-held view that 650-million-year-old rock layers under topsoil can have a much stronger impact on wine and its taste than many believed in the past. The penny had dropped much earlier for Philip, when he was the Core Library Controller at the Department of Mines and Energy. One of his tasks was to clean up the 'ramshackle' system for storing drill core samples from all the mines in the State and, essentially, have the data punched into a computer (under the supervision of Maire Mannik).

'It's a wonderful facility,' Philip says.

> Roxby Downs. All the oil wells. Every water bore. For example, if I want to know whether there's any gold under my house, I hit the computer and access all these drill core samples.
>
> I learned about every inch of the State's geology. Hugh Hudson was the minister. Great, sweet man, tears coming to my eyes. See, Don Dunstan did a really clever thing. He said: 'I'm not going to let any more mining start until we clean up all the sloppy messes that are all over the State. Buy the best set of drilling rigs in the world and drill holes all over this joint. Find out what we've got.' It essentially was a kick in the head to mining companies, you know, you don't just let it slide into the creek.

Philip was bursting with a thirst for knowledge, and it often came to him, or a place nearby. He first heard only the voice of one of his later heroes, David Wynn. A WWII Spitfire pilot, David had made the most of his time in Europe, learning about wine, especially claret.

> I heard him, from my office, at the counter asking for geology maps, different soil types. So I got talking to him and went

driving around with him on a couple of occasions, looking at rocks so I could help him make connections. This was before I was a wine writer. I knew wine was intertwined with the rocks. When David came back from the war, he thought the Coonawarra would make the wines most similar to the great wines of Bordeaux. Its soil. Geology. Thin ferruginous red dirt over the limestone. Very cool. He didn't expect the frosts, which gave him the shits. And he didn't expect that in some years he wouldn't be able to get it right. So, he no longer wanted to do Bordeaux-style wines. He wanted to make Burgundy-type wines like pinot and chardonnay in the Coonawarra. He had the nous to realise it should be done geologically.

The Mines Department was the most amazing place. It had the highest ratio of doctorates of any government department in Australia, under Dunstan. Brains. It was just buzzing. We had the best geological mapping section, it was world famous for accuracy. Billy Fairburn was the scientific editor and his office was next to mine. Billy was a red wine lover and we had this idea that we should do the geology of all wine regions to save them growing grapes in inappropriate locations.

Because, it still happens unfortunately, they try to grow in the easiest places. Flat. Which is not necessarily the best. Billy and I suggested mapping the geology of all the wine regions. We were sort of laughed at – 'Aw, you just want to get on the piss, you know. Why would we bother stuffing around with that when we've just found the biggest uranium deposit in the world at Roxby, and a lot of gold?'

While Philip rarely misses an opportunity to talk about his role in helping Australian winemakers lift their game, there is no doubting his passion and willingness to learn. There was no master plan – just a natural flair for networking, only with a country boy's wonderment. A spooky knack for elegantly stumbling through the crowd and landing at the feet of men or women who could pass on wisdom. One classic example is how much Philip gleaned from a romantic relationship with acclaimed Adelaide chef, Cath Kerry.

> I was fluent in the culinary arts. From 1974 to 1981, these were my almost accidental years of good training. Cath is French–Algerian, so she knew North African food and classical French food very well. She was teaching French at Norwood High School. We'd have dinner parties and people loved to come to them. Five courses, silver service, exquisite food, and I was the waiter.
>
> Wine writers don't spend all their days tasting wine and travelling to easy-on-the-eye destinations, with food to match. But few have the inclination to get among the bristling heat or chill of actual vineyards day after day. Wandering. Wondering. Sniffing. Checking the soil. Hanging around. Asking questions.
>
> Peter Lehmann understood the value of little patches on different grounds. He taught me about wine in society; how it affects the place it comes from and the mentality of those who live in a place by birth. You inherit your grandfather's wine garden and he was in awe of that. He knew the Barossa was special, the quilt, the cornucopia of flavours that you could get because of all those individuals, small holders.
>
> The vine-pull scheme was the big companies trying to clean the Barossa of peasants so they could have Bordeaux-Coonawarra-style viticulture. To bring the costs down.

CHAPTER 17

Fun, Games and Fights: How Philip Knew Legendary Winemakers Better than Anyone

'In front of the Governor-General, he'd grab me by the back of my neck and stick his tongue down my throat.'
– Philip on the late Peter Lehmann

When wine writers – no bigger a cohort than a band of gypsies – complain (understandably) about meagre pay and hard slog, ask them about their junkets. Say, a trip to France, all expenses paid. Listen in, if you can bear it. Nestling on the balcony (think Versailles rather than Buckingham Palace) of a billionaire row chateau central to a French winemaking empire, swigging a glass of red reflecting ghosts all the way back to Napoleon III, who bestowed upon Bordeaux's best wine terroirs the Premier Cru designation.

Four decades ago, Corrine Mentzelopoulos inherited an empire including 1600 grocery stores, a Paris hotel once the home of Louis XIV . . . and a rundown vineyard, Chateau Margaux. Margaux is dilapidated no more. Let's not worry about the vast revenues. 'The light is always different,' waxes the owner. 'I get emotional talking about it.'

With Chinese oenophiles driving demand, first-quarter twenty-first-century wine became the second-best-performing luxury asset, after classic cars, according to property giant Knight

Frank. With new money came opportunity. For overseas junkets, beloved by many writers and journalists.

Philip White was never a fully qualified journalist, any more than he was a fully paid-up geologist. But he did understand the advantage of getting out and about in the real world of a business lauded in the mass media but untouchable to most people. He walked out there in the wind and the dust among the wildest (sometimes broken) dreams of the men and women who had gambled their lives and families on a tiny soft fruit with the temperament of a fifties movie star. He says he holds his head high when it comes to independence.

'I didn't work for anybody I didn't respect. I had a really good job at Orlando then I discovered they'd been making sauvignon blanc out of apple juice and I said, I can't do this, so I walked out,' Philip says. 'I never appeared out front for people.' Like all freelancers, he walks a fine line. Free tickets to countless balls and opening nights, though there was never any direct demand on him to write favourably.

> I've happily knocked trips back if they were smelly. I went to New Zealand once as a guest of the government and that was to do with trade, same with a trip to China organised by the Australian Trade Commission, as a guest of the Chinese government. One of the only real junkets I've been on was as a guest of Frenchman Francois Henry, Australian director of Remy Martin. Krug offered to pay half my airfare. I'd have been pretty stupid to knock that back – it was like going to the Vatican.

Philip forged strong bonds with several leading winemakers. World War II veteran David Wynn: 'A mentor to me, like a grand old man and a good teacher.' Greg Trott. Max Schubert, perhaps the daddy of them all with the thriller-movie-like, secret-stash story of Penfolds Grange. 'Because I was the editor of a national wine magazine, I had access to all these great men,' Philip says.

> The other thing I had going for me was I was the only wine writer really who had journalistic experience. The rest of it was made up of Len Evans and James Halliday, who had wineries and therefore had vested interests. The only other one who was a journo was Huon Hooke.

Then we come to a lump in the throat. Metaphorically, at least, though Philip does get emotional. Peter Lehmann.

> Peter. He had the faith of the growers, he looked after them, made sure they were paid before he got paid. Had their total allegiance. He is why I was so interested to go and live in the Barossa, because of that culture, an amazing thing to have a chance to witness.
>
> It was good when I was there in the eighties because there were still a lot of old people who used to speak the language. There was nothing more educational than sitting on the weighbridge for a day, listening to him talk to every grower. Filling their chit. Weighing their grapes. That community was formidable, in the way that they presumed they would have to rely on each other. Which set me up and no other wine writer was in that position. Peter taught me about resilience and the ability to get back up again in the name of your community.

Philip amplified these thoughts in *InDaily*, following Lehmann's death on 29 June 2013, aged 82.

> Peter's greatest move was not simply his leading of the children of the Barossa, its small grape-growers, on his famous exodus from Saltram after he'd been ordered to cease buying their fruit.
>
> Through those turbulent and treacherous years from the formation of his first redemptive winery, Masterson Barossa

Vineyards, in 1977, until his eventual sale of the majority of Peter Lehmann Wines to Hess Family Estates in 2003, Peter was involved in a constant string of momentous, often desperate, moves to save the growers and therefore the nature of his beloved Barossa from mindless industrial homogeny.

Anybody who witnessed any of those urgent meetings around the Lehmann kitchen table can never forget their intensity.

The combination of full-strength B&H smoke with the fume of burning Mallee roots and redgum in the big fireplace; the table with its books and documents and newspapers; the constant ABC FM music; the endless supply of beautiful red wine, crusty bread and smoked ham; the gathering of those scarce ones with the money; those with the intention and the ideas, and those with nothing more to offer than support and awe at the sheer torque of that collective engine that Peter drove are a set of sensory images that remain etched in the lives of all who were there.

It is difficult to explain the power of forces which worked to clear the Barossa of its peasant-scale grape-growing culture once the big industrialists convinced themselves that their modern trellised monocultural grape yards were capable of replacing any notion of terroir or heritage. Their new version of the science of viticulture would overwhelm any notions so emotive or industrially inefficient and replace them with better returns for their shareholders, at the cost of the very nature of the Barossa and its residents as much as the drinkers.

By the mid-80s, even the government was seduced, and used taxpayer money to pay for the destruction of irreplaceable, invaluable heritage pre-phylloxera vineyards to make way for modern monoculture in what was brutally called the Vine-pull Scheme.

Of the many deserving credit for the final cessation of this destruction, and it was war, none assisted in a more practical manner than Peter, who, through his untiring stubborn determination, schemed and borrowed and strove to keep sufficient money in his coffers to pay these threatened growers for their fruit. Ancient vineyards which now provide the much-modernised Barossa with its international respectability among wine-lovers were saved, leaving the world with a genetic resource and a set of flavours which phylloxera destroyed in Europe.

I loved saving the grenache, too. Because we had a lot of old grenache, which the rest of the world didn't have. When I started that campaign, I was living at the Botanic, in the year 2000 or the next. The price was $250 a tonne when they were pulling it out. Now you get $2500. You can get a lot of fun out of trying to do good things.

I was editing *Winestate*, as a young man. I loved having Peter at my wine tastings when I was too junior to confidently rely on my own judgement. So, soon I became very confident. I was trained by the best men. I loved Lehmann and his cigarettes. Colourful. Raymond Chandler freak, he really thought he was Raymond Chandler. We were drawn to each other. When we were in front of posh people, the Governor-General for example, he used to enjoy saying: 'Oy, Philip, give us a big cuddle.' He'd grab me by the back of my neck and stick his tongue down my throat. He was out there.

Whether with women or men, rampant heterosexual Philip White's most striking relationships have been forged by infinite sparks of passion. He was looking forward to sharing with Lehmann the SA Variety Bush Bash, which took vintage and elderly vehicles 'to places you've never heard of' to raise many millions for children in need.

Philip wrote on drinkster.com:

I'm on the 1988 Burke to Blatherskite Redex Variety Bash, which was mainly conducted in knee-deep mud. Day six and I

> thought there was something bad going on with the 1928 Silver Jubilee Buick. Mick Anderson and Doug Lehmann drove our back-up vehicle through those two weeks of desert downpour; their back-up vehicle had a hammer and a spanner in it, but was mostly laden with wine and beer . . . that remarkable Buick has survived many Bashes . . . and crashes, like when I drove it straight up the arse of Paul Terry's late thirties Rolls Royce limo in the axle-deep mud halfway between Tibooburra and Cameron's Corner . . . you shoulda seen the white plaster bog that fell outta the bum of that Roller, to lie there looking very stark against the red-grey Centralian ooze.

Philip claims Peter Lehmann destroyed the car.

> I stayed at the camp and Lehmann went off in the car. He just went off at two million miles an hour into the bush. Headlights weren't working. The old Buick had broken springs, all bent and twisted. In the morning he was in his swag.

Fellow bashers, including *Advertiser* columnist Alec Mathieson, were surprised to see a noisy conflagration between the winemaker and his co-driver. Philip:

> I hosed down the car. Peter went into the pub. I got the Buick in some sort of order then went looking for Peter. He's in the front bar on his second bottle of gin. I go get him. He came up to me, (yells): 'Whitey. You're trying to take over my team. You're just a little Proddy [Protestant] prick from Kanmantoo, you don't even know who I am.' He was poking his finger in my chest, very aggressively. I considered whether to drop him, which would have been to no avail.
>
> So what did Peter do next? He drank another bottle of gin and everybody was sitting around smoking and looking very embarrassed about it . . . He just drove off. Car looked like a bomb had gone off in it.

> I wanted to write his biography, it would have been a book about how hard it is being the children of preacher fathers. And how that doesn't necessarily equip us for anything. Out in the mud for three weeks and I've got this driver/owner who's off his head. One night the lights went off; the electricity broke in the car. It was terrifying. He wouldn't go any slower than 70 miles an hour.

Philip, with his unique link to darkness in all its manifestations, was clearly traumatised by the journey with one of the closest mates he'll ever have, one with whom he shared secrets that cannot be unbuttoned.

CHAPTER 18

Nosey Parker Bloodhound

'I'm not here to be popular.'
– Philip White, ABC Radio National, 10 June 2011

What makes some experts say Philip is the best wine writer in Australia and among the cream of the rest of the world? First and foremost, he owns what might rudely be known as a great big 'blob'. We all have millions of receptors in our noses, via the olfactory bulb, a blob of nervous tissue where the brain joins the nasal passage. Not very romantic. Far from the popular image of Philip as a towering poet–pirate with boots of Spanish leather and a mesmerising way of storytelling. His nose is a gift and puts him in the same unearthly league as a bloodhound, which can still follow a perfume trail 300 hours old. For the rest of us, that scent disappears in a few minutes. (The king of the animal 'noses' belongs to the African elephant, which combines that blob with a more than handy memory.)

If Philip were simply an in-depth, supernaturally knowledgeable examiner of wine, with all the fine phrases and technical nous, he really would be a footnote. Obvious hallmarks of Philip's character are authenticity, integrity, refusal to bend to commercial or self-interested pressures. But what elevates him, distinguishes him from the crowd, is courage. His battlefield bravery is admired by friends and enemies alike. The courage is linked to truth. You may not agree with the fire and brimstone preached by Philip's pastor father Jimmy, but Jimmy believed in its veracity.

Philip has never been afraid to live a life off the grid. The Kanmantoo Kid was never going to settle down with a wife and three children on a quarter-acre block; regular job, suit and tie. Not for him a 'lifestyle' that has been all but pre-destined, with safety rails and Treasure Island superannuation. More the Neil Young philosophy that life in the ditch can be a lot more stimulating than in the middle of the road.

'He's lived by his own rules,' filmmaker Gus Howard says. 'He's suffered for it and he's had a lot of pleasure from it and he's given a lot of other people pleasure.' Howard says businessmen with an artistic yearning can't simply be artists – they have to build empires, which provides a life with an easily discernible pattern.

> Philip has constantly been writing and rewriting and living his stories. As much as he likes an audience, he creates a wilderness for himself. He's the sort of person who would get a train up to full speed, racing through the night. Jumped out of a lot of runaway trains and cars in his time and been saved because he usually knows when to jump. But there's a litany of self-destruction. So every time he hasn't timed his exit right, it's given him a scar.
>
> He's a very masculine person and men are biologically designed to be self-destructive. So here is a guy who is a stand-up mystical poet. Intelligent, capable, articulate – and he doesn't care. His general vocation is to be some sort of a poet, whether that be some sort of rave poet, vocaliser, behavioural poet or written one who is occasionally supported by work and that has never diminished.

Howard believes one of Philip's striking qualities is his lack of fear.

> He is not scared; he is never timid. But he knows about fears and stands firmly and loudly against them. His father was fearsome. I don't think Philip wanted to personally reject his father, but the man did a pretty good job of creating reasons to be rejected. To all this you add his talent, which he can't escape, and which is driven in a way that seems not to seek at least certain types of reward. He knows his power, but he is not going to use it for power's sake.

If anyone were in any doubt about Philip White's protection racket, that is, protecting his own ferocious independence, they need look no further. Here he is, on ABC Radio National, 10 June 2011: 'I'm not here to be popular.' Hence the willingness to chew the hand that fed him. Railing against a vine-pull scheme that threatened the very fabric of small winemakers, at risk of being swallowed by corporations. Exposing winemakers who were altering their wines in underhanded ways. Pushing for a tax that is fairer to the producers of healthy wines than the cheap cask brigade. And there is always the main attraction: Philip's unique style. 'Sod the wine, I want to suck on the writing,' says D.B.C. Pierre, winner of the Booker and Bollinger Everyman Wodehouse prizes and author of the bestselling novel *Vernon God Little*. 'Probably takes a drink or two to connect like that; he literally paints his senses on the page.'

Philip White also has news for ordinary wine drinkers. He named Butterfly Ridge Riesling in a list of Top 100 wines. It was cheap – $10 a bottle. And now it's not. He introduced readers to Hill of Grace Shiraz when it was $30. Now it's nudging a thousand bucks.

Albert Bensimon says:

> I read that having a good nose is actually having a good memory. It doesn't matter if you know what it smells like, if you don't have a good memory you don't know the individual components. His memory is so good he can remember smelling a saddle thirty-five years ago. And he says, 'That smells like horse saddle.' Wine is the main target. But that nose gives its owner insights limited to a tiny percentage of the population.

Not everyone is a fan of Philip or his work. But there are many happy to place him on a pedestal. If wine writing were a planet, it would be barely visible in the night sky. Tiny. Yet influential, with the moon's ability to pull tides towards one wine trend or another.

Nick Ryan, now with the *Australian*, was thrown out of university but 'used the knowledge from raiding the old man's cellar' to land a job with a wine merchant before moving on to find 'writing was easier than lifting'. Ryan maintains there are two types of wine writer. One is technically very able and reliable but on the pedestrian side: 'Halliday writes like the lawyer he is.' The other breed of scribe, Ryan says, is the equivalent of Neville Cardus on cricket, or Lester Bangs on rock music. They transcend the topic with their allusions, range and style. And an impure lust for the subject. Which brings Ryan to the one he believes tops them all: Philip White. He has been a fan since he was a kid who could only gaze at alcohol from a distance.

> I fell in love with Philip's work before I fell in love with wine. I used to read Philip's tasting notes. They were amazing. Not being a wine drinker at that stage I couldn't quite imagine a liquid in a glass could hold as much as Philip could find in there. You'd read and think: This stuff must be amazing; all this stuff going on in one glass of wine. Australian wine doesn't know how lucky it's been to have Philip chart its progress. If you look at wine writing around the world, there's nothing like Philip. When we

get together the last thing I want to talk about is wine, because he's got such a wide-ranging, curious mind.

Sometimes I think his nose is a blessing and a curse, where his tasting notes are so packed full of ideas. And in newspaper columns especially, it's more about getting quickly to the cheapest wine.

Bensimon believes Philip could have made a fortune from his skills. But he has – wilfully – hobbled along the already rocky, potholed road of the humble freelancer.

He should be a very wealthy man. I've never known him to have the money he deserves. Anyone who is so eloquent and can write so well and have such knowledge of wine. He can write label notes like no one can.

Max Allen is drinks columnist for the *Australian Financial Review*. He came across Philip White in the mid-nineties and follows him still on drinkster.com, which has been running online since 2008. 'Philip's writing, when he is on form, is staggering,' Max says.

It leaves the rest of us for dead. I honestly read the stuff in drinkster.com more than I do any other Australian wine writer. Nobody writes like that, in the same way no one writes like Tim Winton. I can't see the craft. I can't see the thinking behind that sentence, it's working on an emotional level. Philip is the same. And he has stuck to his independent, cranky guns, so it doesn't matter about money. He's been an enormous success.

Max makes a comparison with Gerald Murnane, the loudly lauded but enigmatic Australian novelist.

Hammering away at his novels out in the bush for years. Blithely uninterested in money or commercial success or awards. Yet a lot

> of people think he's the greatest novelist of our generation. If it doesn't matter to you, then you've succeeded.

But Max also recognises the dark side. It lit up around 2012, when natural/alternative wines were on the rise, championed by a newcomer, though hardly a youngster, called Sam Hughes from Sydney. Exhibited the same affinity with language that Philip did. Crazy artist.

'The movement really got under Philip's skin,' says Allen.

> He got rattled, partly because he didn't like the wines – finding them to be sloppy or sub-standard. There was this revolution going on under his nose that he didn't quite get. Or that he got bitter and angry about. He took it out on me for a while. I think the new wave was an extraordinary jab in the arm of the Australian wine industry. Internationally, it had an impact way beyond its actual size.

The tensions bubbled and sizzled at an event in McLaren Vale organised by Amanda Pritchard, creator/director of the Adelaide Food and Wine Festival. Max now reckons Philip was under a misguided impression about the reason for the dinner, where he had been asked to speak. He thought it was to honour renowned Adelaide restaurant critic Howard Twelftree (aka the late John McGrath), who wrote for the *Adelaide Review*, and who Philip worshipped. But Max Allen spoke enthusiastically at the dinner about the new wave of natural wines.

> So there was Philip, in a funk, getting more and more drunk and fuming. He gets up and makes this wonderful, articulate, impassioned speech about Howard. Then, a couple of days later, he has a go at me in a column in drinkster.com, really unnecessarily. Playing the man and not the ball. He was angry. There was some politics involved, I don't know what the story

was. But he wasn't doing himself any favours; coming across as a dinosaur. Yet everyone knows he's got some of the most progressive attitudes. He was out of touch with the movement, though he would argue that he wasn't.

I've seen him write about other people in a similar way. For example, I don't know what's gone on between him and Brian Croser. It was interesting, it told me a lot about the man rather than the writer.

There are public grudges. Also blind spots. I would argue his devotion to Penfolds dates back to Max Schubert. But we've all got favourites and it's almost impossible not to. Philip doesn't hide that.

CHAPTER 19

How Much is Philip White Worth?

'Philip's very good at holding a grudge and recalling all the people he does not agree with.' – Milton Wordley, photographer

How can we judge the weight of Philip White, his value to the wine industry? Who really knows the answer? It is difficult to deny Philip was a man for his times and for the supremely gifted winemakers who made a big impression. He had a better idea of which way the wind was blowing than his older, far more conservative rivals; and was able to change tack. He was listening and watching and checking and observing in a brand-new way.

Accomplished youngster Brian Croser, one of the first in Australia to suit grape vines to regions and who championed premium wines – a category essential to triumphs overseas – would know Philip's value to the wine industry. Another was Wolf Blass, hired to make sparkling wines for Kaiser Stuhl that could compete with the infamous Barossa Pearl, which helped wean drinkers off soft drinks in the fifties and sixties. Soon, he was making red wines drinkable without extended ageing, a breakthrough. Never one to let his thick German accent smother publicity opportunities, Blass quickly gained a reputation. It was whispered he paged himself at airports so his name would be heard. Rumoured that he drove his Rolls Royce into a stobie pole, throwing a suburb into darkness before disappearing, clutching personalised number plates. This realm of misbehaving, groundbreaking eccentrics and individualists perfectly suited Philip. His humming curiosity silenced any judgemental side. And he was as excited about bending the rules as anyone.

In the 1970s and 1980s, wine writers tended to be older. Conservative. Suits and bushy eyebrows and pleasantries and ordinary prose. Like James Halliday, a lawyer, who wrote with knowledge slowed by a stiffness of style. Or Len Evans, an Englishman who became the first regular wine columnist in Australia in 1962. Along came Philip White. Long black hair. Tight jeans. Fancied himself as a lookalike of Gram Parsons, the American country rock music pioneer with a heavy drug habit and a disturbingly mysterious death in the Mojave Desert that was marked in a U2 album, *The Joshua Tree*. His coffin was stolen, then set on fire, but only partially.

'I was a punk, nothing like wine writers were,' Philip says. By 1980, he was 'the biggest wine writer in the country' in the *National Times*. The national weekly newspaper won many awards for its investigative journalism. It famously leaked details of the Costigan Royal Commission into the Painters and Dockers Union, implicating a prominent businessman codenamed 'The Goanna'. The rough-edged Kanmantoo Kid with a streak of poetry was getting rave reviews.

Blass is up there in the pantheon of winemakers – no question. And Philip got to know them all.

> Along with highly competitive mates like Ray Beckwith, Max Schubert and David Wynn, Ian Hickinbotham was a vital, incredibly influential cornerstone of the Australian wine of today. Internationally, it's impossible to measure the impact of

> Hick's work – with Beckwith's newfound knowledge and David Wynn's support – had on the, er, ahem, little matter of malolactic fermentation, just for starters.

Outspoken and fearless, White loved stomping all over Australia, poking bubbles of runaway ego.

With Philip's gold came a special grip on grudges. One of his best friends and helpers is photographer Milton Wordley, son of social conscience journalist Dick Wordley. He believes:

> Philip's very good at holding a grudge and recalling all the people he does not agree with. Insiders speak in awe of the war waged, between the lines, against people such as Brian Croser, who once hired Philip as a consultant.
>
> When we had finally printed the first edition of *A Year in the Life of Grange*, Philip and I and the book's designer, John Nowland, agreed we would give a few signed copies to friends and clients. We sat down in the Crafers pub to sign the books and got to the one both John and I planned to give to our client Brian Croser. We told Philip, this one's for Brian, it's up to you if you sign it. Philip signed it and when we gave it to Brian, he asked us to tell Philip that while they had not been the best of friends, for many years he considered Philip to be one of the best wine writers around and he always enjoyed reading everything he wrote. Interestingly, when Langtons had the fundraising auction for Philip, Brian donated a case of wine as did many others who had felt Philip's lash. Says a lot about the respect he has in the wine trade.

Geoff Merrill, big of hair, moustache and personality, was a man for the eighties. Drove glammed-up, souped-up Holdens. Became mates with English cricketing superstars Ian Botham and the late Bob Willis, some of whose ashes were released in McLaren Vale. Merrill, though, was no 'rock star' lightweight. More than a thousand medals, a Jimmy Watson trophy and international recognition via appointments as consultant to large enterprises. From Philip's own pen:

> As I sort through a lifetime of notebooks, papers, photographs and diaries in the hope of building a decently researchable archive, I'm finding some true morsels. Like this account of a tasting Geoff Merrill staged to promote his spendy new 1996 McLaren Vale Shiraz.
>
> With alarming generosity, in 2001 Merrill flew the hackpack into Melbourne and poured his wine, blind, along with the most buzzy, extravagant Shiraz bottles of the day. Wines he obviously imagined he could match. After we'd all done our notes, he pulled the bags off the bottles and we added their names to our appraisals. I reckon there were about a dozen wine scribes in attendance.
>
> Being a foolhardy sort of a bloke, Merrill didn't seem to contemplate the chance that we'd prefer other more famous wines over his own. Which we did.
>
> Merrill's 1996 Henley Shiraz was awarded 75 points; Henschke's 1996 Hill of Grace got 80. Nothing amiss, there.

Whatever the nuances, top winemakers respected his opinions, though some walked a fine line when discussing their relationship, personal and professional. One of Philip's strengths has been getting the dust of many wine regions on his boots. That meant he knew what was going on behind the scenes – which press releases were overblown and who was resting too much on their laurels, or adding unsuitable substances to their product. He made dozens of firm friends. Some became enemies, to varying degrees. I'd say there is no love lost between Blass and Philip, though they shared fun, intimate times as they sped around the countryside, intimidating fences, in Blass's Merc. Last time I spoke to Blass, at an Adelaide Wine Centre function, he felt he lost Philip because he (Blass) was making too much money. Philip talks about Blass with affection, tinted with cynicism. The motormouth immigrant with the bow ties, a Rolls Royce penchant and a Trabant twang was brought over from Germany to SA to find wines to compete with Barossa Pearl, a much-scorned but popular, cheap sweet sparkling white wine credited with weaning teenagers off soft drink. That offer came from Kaiser Stuhl's Ian Hickinbotham, a restlessly innovative winemaker who came up with a world-first solution for preventing oxidation during the making of sparkling wine.

In 1951, Hickinbotham was only the thirty-fifth qualified winemaker to emerge from what was then Roseworthy Agricultural College. It pained him that the community at large had mainly disdain for his craft, a thorn that motivated his inventive streak. It helped none that the industry was insular and ultra-conservative. When he perfected the 'bag in a box' in the mid-sixties, Hickinbotham's bosses at Penfolds took no notice, as they were much more worried about the dwindling sales of Royal Reserve Port.

Philip shortcuts Hickinbotham's brief to Blass: *Get rid of all the sultanas and all the shit grapes. Make money.*

Philip:

> Wolfie was a businessman but he also understood how to make drinks. And what he taught me was how to respond to the market. Like, one year, something must have gone wrong in their office and I got a set of samples from each of their Australian offices: Brisbane, Sydney, Melbourne, Adelaide and Perth. The biggest selling white wine in Australia then was Yellow Label Riesling. I discovered they were all different, had different sweetness. So Wolfie was selling a different product to each

city, dependent on that city's palate. Like, Brisbane was very ignorant in wine, so that was sweet. They were pissed off about my revelations, a nightmare from a company perspective, it was a big mistake sending me that selection of wine. I was always in awe of Wolf's ability to set new styles according to what he thought the public wanted. He was called a blender. He was very successful. Until he bought Quelltaler Wines at Clare to get riesling, he didn't have a winery. Then I discovered when I went to live in Greenock, in my Barossa days, that a blender was patois for a consultant who steals wine from their clients and blends it. The first Blass wines were pinched from Normans.

CHAPTER 20

Blunt Honesty Hurts

'Philip's gift to you is his honesty. You want the truth? Talk to Philip. He'll tell you for free.'
– Leon Bignell, local MP and former State ALP minister

One of Philip's most ardent admirers is Leon Bignell. 'Biggles' – as he is known – won the seat of Mawson in 2006 and was delighted to find a sharing of common ground – a desire to protect the agricultural status of the vineyards of McLaren Vale and the Barossa.

But epic as it was, that battle faded into insignificance towards the end of 2018 when Philip was in poor health and Biggles was far from alone in his fear that Philip might not see that Christmas. He had visibly altered. The powerful frame of a classic six-footer was not quite so imposing. While he somehow managed to retain his unique, knee-tilting, long-legged gait, the energy loss was confronting. His stomach was boiling with tumours. A nasty piece of cancer was burrowing its way along his spine into his brain. And his groin was 'melting'. If there was going to be a solution, it wasn't going to be any fun.

Given Philip's bucolic surroundings in a picturesque cottage at Yangarra Estate Vineyard, his condition seemed all the more unfair. You could sit all day on the veranda, overlooking hills rolling to the coast. Watching the magpie that's been thrown out of its nest and has been struggling along because no one likes it. The kangaroos. The rabbits. Drinking in peace and serenity. Broken maybe by the thump-whump of hares mating and fighting and mating out front. A glass of one of Philip's obscure but cunningly good wines in your hand. His words flowing into your ears, filled with original thoughts. Funny stories. Everybody was talking about The End. Out of Philip's earshot. Only one person – from among a crowd of loyal, truly loving friends – was brave enough to discuss the cold, hard truth with Philip. Biggles was on the veranda as the November sunshine faded into night.

'It wasn't a night of throwing back drinks,' he recalls.

> It was a very measured quiet night, a few glasses of wine, a beer then a scotch. I said, 'Who knows what you want to happen once you're not here?' Silence. Philip covered his face and made an indecipherable noise. How upset was he going to be, this soft but loud man who never disguised a single emotion?

Biggles: 'First question – cremation or burial?'

To his credit, Philip seemed to snap out of the initial shock of such a barefaced, ungilded challenge. He responded. 'I don't really know, Biggles, that's a bit deep.' Biggles told Philip he remembered him saying he'd like to be buried in the same place as winemaker Greg Trott. 'Oh yeah, Biggles, imagine that. Me and Trotty rolling underground in the Strout Road Cemetery.' Biggles smiles. 'It turned out to be a beautiful night, actually. We talked about music and he showed me all the instruments he's collected. He's not a flashy man.'

Back to the hard chat about the unmentionable.

Biggles: 'Second question – you're not a marble headstone sort of guy, so what rock do you want?'

Philip: 'It's got to be local slate. And with one line of inscription – can you guess what?'

Biggles: 'No.'

Philip: 'WHAT ARE YOU LOOKING AT?'

While a team of Flinders Medical Centre specialists has had to wage the cancer battle on Philip's behalf, he has never been afraid to enter a struggle that he can influence. Plenty of environmental yarns have the wine writer climbing out of his bottle-fed comfort zone and leading a charge against developers. One was fought in McLaren Vale to stop the urban sprawl. The eventual result was the *Character Preservation Act*. 'Philip was one of the driving forces,' Leon Bignell says.

> I found in Philip a great ally. I trusted every bit of advice he gave me. Having people like him around gave you the kind of energy that you needed to fight the fight. Not everybody in the government at the time felt the same way as I did. I've always said: 'He knows more stuff about more stuff than anyone I've ever met in my life.' And he's generally on the side of right, as well. Not someone who wants to blow smoke up your arse and gain some benefit from their view. He doesn't care about that. He'll do anything to make sure the right thing is done. Unfortunately too few politicians get to hang out with people like him. They hang out with themselves. All politicians should have mentors who are as alert to the political system as Philip is.

Bignell, a former news reporter, could easily be mistaken as a relative of Philip's. A nephew, maybe. The son Philip never had. He's got a similar air – rambunctious, opinionated, earthy and highly intelligent. Knows how to find the bottom of a beer or wine glass. Has a generosity of spirit. Stays on the right side of the law, but can't help peeking over to the other side to see what's happening.

> The great thing about representing McLaren Vale is there are some thoughtful people down there. So we sat around having meetings with butcher's paper saying, 'What is it we want this place to look like in 100 or 150 years' time? What sort of protections do we need in place that will prevent the area from turning into a Seaford or any other suburb in SA?' Philip was a big part of that. And the man pushing Philip along was the late Greg Trott, winemaker. Through Trott, Philip knew all of those stories and the importance of preserving agricultural land.
>
> I was getting supercharged by Philip and other people from McLaren Vale and the Barossa. That brought about the *Character Preservation (Barossa) Act 2012* and the *Character Preservation (McLaren Vale) Act 2012*. We copied the example of Napa Valley wine region in California in 1968. Now those two areas are locked in forever, in the same way Colonel Light did with the Park Lands surrounding the city of Adelaide.

'Politics,' says Biggles, 'had nothing to do with it. Like Philip, Trott was a larger-than-life eccentric who loved his local region. From the grave he's saying: "You boys are doing all right because from a political point of view no one was doing any work on it."'

The way Leon Bignell sees it, one of Philip White's several gifts is an ability to explain his knowledge of complex information in simple ways, easily understandable to the layperson. Philip has made on-the-run mentoring his own art form.

> He explains the whole character preservation movement against the backdrop of local history. He goes back to the Indigenous people of the area and their stories, and how important it is to preserve them. It's invaluable what he's taught me. He's a very smart man, he knows the ways to achieve what's right for the local area, the State, the nation.

Biggles, like many, reckons Philip White is on the genius spectrum. Somewhere. If most of us mere mortals manage to retain thirty per cent of what we've learned, that's a bonus. Philip is retaining a hundred per cent of everything he's tasted or drunk, or smelled or listened to. It is also the case that more than one of Philip's mates has noted in passing that he has 'pissed off a lot of people in his time'. Biggles ventures that Philip's intense and dogmatic demeanour is open to misinterpretation, particularly by those who have only recently made his acquaintance. 'It takes a bit to get behind the Philip thing and he can come across as grumpy and combative,' Biggles says.

> You've got to know how to work with him. Sometimes we've had a conversation and you can see it going down a certain track where he's getting upset. But at the end of the day it's not important to our relationship. You have to be attuned to his eyes and the pitch in his voice, and you just go wherever the conversation goes.
>
> I'm sure there are people all over SA and further afield who think that Philip doesn't like them. It springs from him giving an honest appraisal of whatever the subject is, wine or anything else. Here's this poor bastard who thinks for ten years that Philip thinks he can't make wine or is a loser. Yet Philip has been praising that winemaker to his friends. It's what makes it so special when Philip does say something nice to you or about you. Because when he delivers the message it's come through such a deep thought process.
>
> He was pretty devastated about what happened around Mt Barker and the subdivisions in the fields he'd have grown up around. When you listen to Philip talk about geology, he says there are rock formations you see in the Flinders that go way down deep underground and pop up again at Hallett Cove. He's very in tune with the environment around him.

One of the best things is taking him for drives. We'll drive past standard trees that I've driven past thousands of times and he'll tell me why they are important, why they are protected. And then he goes, 'See those rocks, they were either dropped there by aliens or some higher force, or there was some big mountain range here because they do not belong in this area.' Philip will tell the story of why vegetation was planted along the roads, because the leaves contain an antiseptic and there's a big stem that comes up the top of them and when you pull up your horse, they were like first aid stations all along the highways. The stem had a thread that already had antiseptic qualities and you could use it to stitch up wounds.

CHAPTER 21

The Hotel Conversational

'We got rid of the pool table. The television. People said to me: "You'll go broke."' – Nick Binns, ex-owner, Exeter Hotel

It is no small irony that a man who vowed never to chase money, let alone wealth, became a successful 'brand' – call it happenstance, accident, whatever moved in the cosmos. But Philip White is credited with playing a substantial role in the rise in the popularity of the Exeter Hotel on Rundle Street. His contribution is difficult to measure, because Nick Binns and his brother bought the Exeter seven months before a major addition to Adelaide's social calendar; the Australian Formula One Grand Prix. Its high-octane glamour brought a new world of international superstars to the city, and the rundown Rundle Street got a turbo charge that boosted every single business around. However, it was a mixture of fortuitous happenings that made the Exeter special among hundreds of hotels. One was the regular presence of the punk-pop band Exploding White Mice, which reportedly took its name from a movie in which a laboratory mouse exploded when exposed to music by The Ramones. Binns recalls: 'They really made the Exeter take off in those early days. They got us on the map, playing in the front room. That was one side of it, attracting the young alternative kids.'

The other side was Philip. He was ear-catching. Brimming with knowledge to share, and a touch of the Viking that made him dangerously interesting. Women certainly saw that kind of forbidden promise. It was as if he was a fully paid-up entertainer, reminiscent of storytelling Peter Ustinov at his best, plus a Gordon Ramsay splash, but spontaneously presenting a free performance. Standing, not beside the counter of the front bar, but just far enough back that a circle of interested punters could gather around him. And, by the way, talk back. Ask questions. Even heckle, though that could be risky. Philip had a lashing tongue, and was never keen on backing down in an argument.

When he built up a bit of verbal steam, when he floated into a zone, he could be mesmerising. An orator. Voice rising and falling in a deliberate, theatrical way. The boy who did his pastor father's bidding and preached the Old Testament on the main street of Murray Bridge had become the man who parlayed that fire and brimstone into inspirational, free-form discourse. This show attracted an unusually wide assortment of drinkers. Many of them shared Philip's curious nature, and were looking for fresh sensations, meaty conversations.

On the flipside, several close mates say Philip can be mouthy and provocative, to a scary extent. 'I tended to get into biffo a lot,' Philip says:

> which is one of the reasons I have brain troubles now. I don't recall ever starting a fight but I'd wade in. Or I'd be too easy to hit by an idiot, you know. It took a few years to get that out of the system. It wasn't the savage violence you see these days, with head kicking and all that. Getting away from violence was a long, slow thing. While I kept finding myself wounded physically from stupidity, not to mention motorbike and car accidents and getting

pissed and all that silliness, that reinforced my suspicion that I was correct in not having children.

Medical evidence places Philip in the league of AFL and NFL footballers whose lives have been shredded by head clashes. Even so, he can still hold his own with remarkable resilience – another X in the Philip factor. It is hard, however, to breathe in the ashes of the sheer number of hits and broken bones. Philip can list at least twenty-two serious concussions, due to everything from car and motorcycle accidents to assault, resulting in a daunting diagnosis of permanent traumatic brain injury (TBI) and dementia pugilistica (a subgroup of chronic traumatic encephalopathy (CTE)), and persistent shorter-term post-concussion syndrome (PCS) complicated by post-traumatic stress disorder (PTSD).

Mark Thomson is one of many men and women drawn into Philip's orbit by his intellect and stimulating conversation – rather than his derring-do. An event from more than thirty years ago, outside the Exeter Hotel, has entered folklore. It remains shrouded in the mists of time for most. Except for Mark, who was only feet away from the carnage. It seemed like bad timing for a stranger resembling a small bikie to choose that Friday night to perch on the vinyl roof of Philip's treasured blue Valiant, a lovingly rejigged, roaringly powerful ex-police car.

Mark recalls:

> I was out the front of the Exeter when he got whacked by the bikie. Right next to him. It happened so fast. What I can still recall, and it was sickening, was the sound of Philip's head hitting the road. He fell over backwards. It was like a watermelon, that sound.

It's a laughing matter now, but the weapon that abruptly came into play was a small, pink rolling pin attached to a press release, used to promote a bakery. Philip had been carrying it around, for reasons unknown. Mark believes his mate had been mouthing off at the 'bikie' (no one can confirm the stranger's affiliations), being bumptious, 'in full floral mode'.

> I do remember the bikie not being a scary-looking guy at all. In one motion, took less than a second, he grabbed the tiny rolling pin from Philip and whacked him. He was only a little guy. But very quick. Bang. I remember thinking: Philip doesn't understand what fighting is actually like because this guy had no hesitation about resorting to violence. And two women cops on horseback came up . . . somebody had run up and told them someone had just been assaulted and they galloped down Union Street. It was so bizarre, they were asking: What's going on? Philip was all floppy.

Philip has his own recollections of the incident. He'd been working during the day at the Formula One Grand Prix on Friday, 13 November 1987. Later, he was in the Exeter playing darts with a group of winemaker mates. Outside was his pride and joy, a souped up ex-police Valiant hot rod.

> I left to go home for dinner when I saw this bloke, Tyrone, sitting on the roof of my car. He and his friends were very friendly, and I showed them over the vehicle.
>
> Then Tyrone accuses me of threatening him with a screwdriver – bullshit. He slid off the roof and headbutted me. Splattered my nose all over my face. Claimed I'd accused him of disrespecting my car. I'm holding him off with the darts I still have in my hand. Then he jabbed me several times in the head with the rolling pin. I overheard the ambulance crew talking about how my heart stopped at one stage. The shirt I was wearing was soaked in blood. He was hissing at me when I was trying to give evidence in court. He got 30 months in jail. The best witness

> I had was an old Latvian lady who saw the whole incident with her husband and who said of the assailant: 'And after he had done it to him, he looked like he'd won a gold medal for Australia.'

Nowhere is it recorded that, in the course of his adult life, Philip started a fight in a physical way, and finished it cleanly. Any tales are of Philip on the wrong end of a melee, having usually entered the fray to try to prevent further damage. What people do discuss is Philip's lashing tongue. Tubby Justice says he'd get into trouble because he was so good at verbal gymnastics that blokes would get frustrated and land a punch on him. 'No one could ever beat him in an argument,' she recalls.

'I've always been interested in obscure, cultural stuff and Philip was a person I could speak to,' says Thomson, an eccentric, inventive brainbox.

> We're a couple of know-alls, out-knowing each other. He knew who the Wendish people were in the Barossa. They are supposedly one of the lost tribes of Israel. They were cast out of Germany and came here as part of the Silesian immigrant scheme and they lived on the margins of Barossa society and (according to Philip) were not widely trusted. They were farmers, mainly. Wendt, Lehmann, Noack and Modra are some of the several distinctive Wendish names. Often very good sports people.
>
> That's the kind of obscure topic Philip and I would discuss. Or the very furthest niches of country and western music.

Nick Binns, when publican at the Exeter, observed Philip up close over many years and never saw a violent side. 'I never had to throw Philip out,' he laughs.

> But I had to save him once when he got hit by that bikie. Blood everywhere. Probably everyone was pissed and someone said the

wrong thing. I went to grab some tea towels and yelled to one of the staff members: 'Not the good ones!'

As to the timing of the purchase of the Exeter, Binns is happy to admit he and his brother got lucky. 'We didn't know that car race was coming – I was never into that sport,' he says.

> We'd sold another pub and a supermarket and hadn't worked for five months. So we bought the Exeter for $90,000 and put three years on the lease. My brother said, 'Well we'll get our money back and we can earn money on the way through.'

And Binns doesn't pretend he had any pre-set big ideas for the Exeter.

> I didn't do anything; I just sold the booze to the customers. We had a few rules that obviously they liked and we did a few things that encouraged people to come, including an unusual number of maverick lawyers, unusually interesting accountants and misfit businessmen. Non-mainstream.
>
> I remember we started off pouring West End Draught. After about five or six years, we ventured into selling Coopers – it all happened with their Pale Ale.

In fact, the switch to the local Coopers brewery – a forerunner to the new wave of craft beers that followed more than a decade later – made it much easier to identify trouble-prone clients. There were a few rules: no exposed tattoos, no blue singlets, no steel-capped boots. 'They'd come in with their shorts and singlets, complaining that we didn't serve West End beer,' Binns chuckles. 'We'd say: "That's right, so off you go." Problem solved.'

The peeled-paint-and-dowdy look gave the Exeter an edge, when a parallel trend was to flash up hotels, with polished timber and shiny brass, like the nearby Earl of Aberdeen. 'It was Keep It

Simple, Stupid,' Binns says.

> We got rid of the pool table. The television. Took a couple of years to do it. People said to me: 'You'll go broke.' And I said, 'Well, how does that affect you? That's my problem, what are you worried about?' Eventually, it became obvious we didn't need any of these outside things to make it successful. The people who came didn't want to watch TV. For every one that left because of no pool table or TV, another three came in. It was a true conversational pub. That wasn't necessarily our intention. It simply evolved. Every alteration I had in the pub was subtle. Changed the whole front counter one Sunday night, people came in the next day and didn't notice anything.
>
> The people who populated the pub pushed it in various directions. I have nothing against pokies; they weren't for that pub. Like the Austral was never going to be a pokies pub. I've got about ninety pokies at other pubs, Robin Hood, Glynde and Gawler. I don't tell people how to spend their money. The Grand Prix did expose the East End to a new bunch of people. That was just cream on the top because it was only Wednesday until Sunday night. But it was huge. It helped pay for new machinery, upgrades, it created enormous cash flow.

The five days around the street race were crazy. Rundle Street was a noisy place at the best of times, but the social revellers' clock turned upside down during the week of visiting legends like Alain Prost, the late Ayrton Senna and George Harrison – a massive revhead. Busy became frantic. Binns, who eventually found the scene too much to handle and retired early at fifty-three in 2000, remembers:

> Three o'clock in the morning, wheeling cans of beer over to Ruby's Cafe to put it in their cold room to try getting it ready before it all started again in a few hours. Then back to the Exeter

by six o'clock to make breakfast for the interstate guests who were working on the Grand Prix.

Ruby's Cafe had long been a bastion of the area, and was getting another shot in the arm from the GP. As did Gladys Sym Choon, which began in 1928 as a mini-emporium and was later taken over by Joff Chappell and fashion designer Razak. Journalist Colin James knew Philip in the early nineties when he shifted back into the city from Kanmantoo, following a stint looking after his ageing parents. 'He'd become very isolated because he stopped driving,' James says.

> Moving brought him back to the city and the Botanic, which was only a stone's throw from his spiritual home, the Exeter. The Exeter, walking back in there today after first seeing it in 1988. Same colour. Still the same kinds of patrons. Only back then, you could cut a knife through the smoke in the front bar. You could order a bottle of Krug, $100 a bottle, it was just there, all the rich guys at the Exeter. This was the original hipster's joint before they were even born. Philip was probably the original hipster. Philip was always so protective of Rundle Street – he hated all the demolitions, the East End markets getting knocked over and he didn't like the Maris family [of property developers] takeover.

Although Philip White was upset about some of the local development, he had become a good-luck charm for the Exeter. More evidence of the Midas touch came after Binns placed the highly regarded wine writer in charge of the Exeter's wine list. 'He was a huge factor in the hotel, doubling its turnover in three years,' Binns says. Before that appointment, Binns was continually being ticked off by customers who would look at a $37 bottle of wine on his shelves and complain they could get it for $15 at a liquor store.

> What Philip did was bring in wines that were different to the norm. They were hard to find, alternative, so people couldn't compare prices like they used to with the popular brands. And people loved Philip's wines. He also had a group of friends who used to drink at the British. One by one, they came over to the Exeter. Philip was very generous with his time and he used to arrange meetings with all the winemakers at the Exeter. He used to do the Top 100 Wines for the *Advertiser*. And every year they'd have a Citizens' Tasting Panel. Philip would come in and throw money on the bar and bring a whole lot of people.

The serendipitous largesse didn't stop there. When Philip co-founded a renegade petanque club based in the nearby eastern Park Lands, their regular Sunday lunches were on the balcony of the Exeter. Friends say Philip is not a leader in the classical sense. No arm waving or barking. But any bystander who witnessed Philip White at the head of that group as it made its way along Rundle Street was unlikely to be in any doubt as to who was the guiding light.

CHAPTER 22

Pernod and Petanque

'We call Pernod the throwing juice. So that's sometimes how we play: a glass of Pernod in one hand, ball in the other.'
– Chris Crago, former petanque club member

When it came to adulthood and freedom to choose a sport, it's instructive that Philip's choice was petanque. And it is even more telling that it was Philip who corrupted the rules. Thus, what could seem like a pretentious embrace of a French game for non-athletes (invented by a Jules Lenoir to get around his rheumatism) was turned into faintly reckless anarchy. Add the fact that a player was allowed to play while holding a glass of a potent drink (that replaced the banned absinthe) in one hand and ball in the other and you get the full Philip picture. Absinthe – wicked nectar for the romantic poets! A sly yet playful humour. Imposing himself without hurting anyone. It's a wonder they didn't go the whole hog and name the heavily adapted game after Philip.

Thus was born the Feral Aussie Boullistes Club in the East Park Lands, about 300 metres from the Exeter on Rundle Street. The official launch was by Lord Mayor Henry Ninio, on 11 December 1994, at the FAB Petanque Boulledrome. In the early days, up to seventy people – most of whom had never thought of hiring a tailor or fashionista – gathered to play. The prize was a modest amount of cash and a bottle of wine. Plus, much to the astonishment of habitués who regarded Exeter publican Nick Binns as the meanest man in town, a free lunch in his establishment. That, and the fact the club was only formed so members could play in the next Australian Championships, scheduled to be played in Adelaide soon after, marks the end of formality.

Veteran player, one-time club official and communications consultant Chris Crago tried to help a bewildered James Plummer, of ABC Radio National, through an interview during a game in January 2000. 'We have a few rules,' she explained. 'But they're spoken rules and we agree on things. If someone wants to throw a certain length, the other people can agree it's okay to do that.'

Plummer was still off-balance, surrounded by 'athletes' who either looked – to him – like James Dean in leather or Barry Humphries clones. He persisted: 'You don't actually have anything marked out . . . people are almost standing shoulder to shoulder, playing separate games. It's anarchy, really.' Chris: 'We're feral, you just have to find your spot and stick to it.' She recalls a trip to Melbourne that consolidated the push to form FAB. 'Pernod sponsored a bus for us to travel there, and supplied refreshments along the way, and Nick Binns supplied our food for the trip. The event was even a feature spread in *Vogue* magazine.'

History explains why this particular corner of Rymill Park so suited the disdain for decorum. The Park Lands were the first of their kind, in 1837, as part of the best-planned nineteenth-century city in the world. Such spaces had – until then – been reserved for royalty and other wealthy landowners.

'Philip was known by many in the club, mainly women, as "The King",' says journalist Lance Campbell, one of a handful of remaining original members.

> This was because of his size and bearing which includes his Henry VIII head. It could also be because he dispensed largesse in the form of innumerable tasting bottles of wine – opened but with only a small amount of the contents missing – to the FAB masses on many Sunday mornings.

As with so much else involving Philip White, the petanque adventures had their genesis over drinking sessions in the front bar of the Exeter Hotel. It was a good way to ease into Sunday under the shadows of a hangover. Set among gorgeous, towering gum trees, the petanque park is an ideal place for resetting the sight of sore eyes. In the moments of non-action (and there are a few) a Saturday night reveller can listen to the astonishingly varied melodies of the scores of different varieties of birds. Magpies and their sometimes rowdy rituals are a free show in themselves, the strutting males having perfected the airs of a puffed-up, well-fed, long-coated aristocrat from the nineteenth century. You can watch the splashes of living, darting art that are the corellas, feeding on titbits from the abundant larder of trees.

Chris Crago was there with FAB from the start, though she no longer participates. 'Many of us, myself included, had been out all night, and made it to petanque the next morning . . . then went to lunch at the Exeter.' One of the unifying juices for a disparate bunch of bohemians was a common love of exceptionally good food and drink. Chris Crago again:

> At that time, Ted Pettifor was working at Orlando, which was owned by Pernod-Ricard, and he was keen to promote these brands. So we had our first sponsor, who made sure we had plenty of Pernod and Ricard to drink. And Pernod T-shirts, flasks, glasses and umbrellas, plus our Pernod cart, which was a standout feature on the piste every Sunday.

Our opening day was very memorable. Philip had been reviewing wines for his annual review, so he had many leftover bottles for tasting in the day. We all called on our food and wine contacts for our opening party, which set the bar for our FAB events. Peter Darley had his Oyster Bar, so supplied a sack of oysters to be freshly shucked, and renowned Exeter chef Libby Martin and her sister Helen prepared a magnificent feast, along with all the winemakers who donated wines for the day.

Our AGMs were also legendary events, back in the days when we were all more carefree, so everyone came along, determined to have a good time.

One of FAB's annual events is named for its most flamboyant member, the late Christos Juhanson, also one of the best players. He stood out like a human rainbow in the crowd of rugged, battered individualists – droll lawyers and real-estate agents, painters, chefs, winemakers, alcoholic gardeners. Yellow hair. A frivolous, camp-but-straight cross-dresser, Christos had the wardrobe of a gypsy-cum-hippy-cum-punk. The energy of a jumping jackrabbit. Had a permanent look in his eyes that reminds of singer Rod Stewart when he's about to say something naughty. Always on the precipice of mischief.

You'd be hard-pressed to find anyone around the Adelaide East End who did not love Christos, who married five times (twice to the same bride).

His early years threw out no clues – his background was in computer programming in the 1960s. 'Christos came to Adelaide as a manager of a computer programming company of about thirty to thirty-five people,' says publisher Michael Zerman.

Coming here from Sydney enabled him to move out of his life as a high-level computer analyst programmer to become the person he became here: a bon vivant, a good chef, a front-of-house person managing venues whether it be a curry night at the Exeter or the bowling club.

'Everybody loved Christos,' recalls Albert Bensimon. 'They had to close off Rundle Street for his funeral procession.' Lance Campbell describes Christos as 'a self-portrait in progress' and, in a 2005 eulogy, 'a tragic loss to the fine art of showing off'. His memory lives on through the Christos Cup: the challenge is to live up to the ghost of the club imperative: Be flamboyant. Eccentric. Kind. Caring and competitive.

Chris Crago, when she was single, once went on a date with Christos, to the Cargo Club to see Zydeco Jump.

> He was wearing his satin green five-piece suit with matching sunglasses, handkerchief, comb, pen and undies, and we had a great night out, and lots of fun. He told me that he was very disappointed that I did not become conquest whatever the number was at the time.

Beyond the merry hedonism of FAB, there is no doubt that the petanque-playing area exists solely because of Philip. It is related to, in no particular order: his insouciant attitude to money; his unique ability to set up a cosmic barter system, underwritten by karma; his bloodless attitude to emotional debates over specific issues.

It was Philip's inimitable criss-crossing of everyday collisions of atoms in the universe that solved a problem that looked too expensive to fix. The human-made lake in the East Park Lands, once used as a kids' wading pool and as a venue to race model speedboats, was an ideal spot for a *piste*. But no one would pay the cost of filling it in. Leon Bignell, ALP Member for Mawson, remembers the story as one that began with Philip as his usual cool-headed self when it came to environmental dramas.

While Philip was a very early 'greenie' and has long been furious about the shenanigans that have for so long crippled the Murray–Darling Basin, he takes each case on its merit. According to Leon Bignell, a stoush over a quarry at Sellicks Caves amounted to nothing of significance. Then writing for the *Advertiser*, Philip declared 'bullshit'. 'I'm all for the environment, sticking up for jewels in our environmental crown, but this is just empty void, little bubbles in the earth's surface,' he thundered. Bignell said the quarry managers appreciated Philip's bluntness and said if ever there was anything they could do for him, please get in touch.

One thing about Philip is it's unconditional that he shows no fear or favour to anyone. He will not be bought at all. But he formed this relationship with the quarry. It did pay dividends down the track when the Adelaide City Council told the would-be pentanque club they'd first have to fill in a pond because of the public liability risk of drowning. At first, the members said they couldn't afford such a project. So Philip says: 'What if you got the dolomite for free?' No one realised how much dolomite it would take – truckload after truckload.

So, to answer the question, was Philip any good at petanque? 'Yes, he was,' says Chris Crago.

> Some of my favourite games were when Jimmy Barker [co-founder of B-Sharp Records] and I played against Philip and Michael Youds [versatile artist and owner of leading man good looks]. We were all of a similar level, so we always had a good and competitive game, with a great outcome, no matter who won.

CHAPTER 23

Philip and the Poet of Darkness

'If you are the dealer, I'm out of the game. If you are the healer, it means I'm broken and lame'
– from 'You Want It Darker', Leonard Cohen

Philip White made a point of going out of his way to meet his musical heroes. Typically, he was unfazed when he attended a Leonard Cohen press conference at Adelaide Airport in 1980, and the sharply dressed poet–songwriter from Montreal asked the media, 'What is netball?' His interest in the sport had been piqued by the sight of an Australian women's netball team on the same plane. 'Amazons,' said Cohen, very much a ladies' man, in that cavernous drawl. 'Amazons.'

Philip remembers:

> Leonard sat in a low-slung chair, dressed in an impeccable black suit and white shirt, no necktie. Black crocodile country boots. There were the usual questions, such as: 'Do you still drop acid when you write songs?' I asked him what it was like working with Phil Spector. At which point, he asked me: 'Do you know a bar?'
>
> So, off we went. He really enjoyed stories about what his image was in Adelaide. I told him about the time the poets Allen Ginsberg and Lawrence Ferlinghetti came here and we were in a house in Mylor and I played them Leonard's latest album, *Songs of Love and Hate*. They couldn't believe they hadn't heard it before and couldn't understand why we got it first here in Australia.

While the late Cohen displayed a wonderfully dry humour in performance, his songs were often lyrically beautiful but downbeat – some say he was a man of constant sorrow. His much-covered secular hymn 'Hallelujah' was far from his only venture into religion. Not long before he died, Cohen composed 'You Want It Darker', a song that mixes accusation with despair. According to filmmaker Gus Howard, Philip has an obsession with the spiritual element of darkness.

Dr Malka Simkovich, an authority on Catholic–Jewish studies in Chicago, argues:

> When it comes to human beings causing people harm in the manner of God, Cohen lays the responsibility for human evil at God's feet: If you wanted things different, God, you would have made it so. Cohen's confession that he didn't know he had 'permission to murder and to maim' suggests that people are killing others in God's name, using their faith as a means to justify violence. Cohen surrenders to a relationship in which he will forever be in the dark – because that's how God wants it.

For some reason, Philip was not as open about his dealings with Cohen as he was about other stars. Perhaps he regarded their private conversations as somehow sacred. His brief summation: 'A very wise man, somebody you could respect.'

Philip White has always been eager to distance himself from the Holy Trinity:

> I took a lot of acid in those early days. Three years of acid. Like sometimes two tabs a week. In retrospect I realise it was a purgative and it was very convenient for removing all the Jesus out of my blood. I'm living proof that Jesus leads straight to acid.

CHAPTER 24

Standing Up for the Little Guys

'He does not like the big guys screwing over the little guys.'
– Colin James, journalist

Philip White is held in high regard by his peers, who give him credit for saying what he thinks regardless of the casualties, even when they include himself. Journalist David Sly, a widely read food and wine critic, spent years editing Philip's copy for the *Advertiser* in the nineties. 'Philip's a polarising character, because he is very absolute,' Sly says.

> His command of language is so formidable. There can be a real viciousness to his words. Philip had so many detractors. So many times at functions, somebody who had been blowtorched by Philip's column would march up to me, finger jabbing my breast-bone demanding that Philip get removed from the pages. It was really confrontational stuff. Wineries, marketers. An army of enemies gathering outside. That gave me more belief in Philip, because a couple of those finger-pointers turned out to be rogues in the long run. They came undone so I look back and smirk on that because they were very self-righteous. Felt their reputations had been bruised. He'd lambast Coonawarra as a district for over-irrigating their vines and that would get the entire community inflamed with loathing until he'd find one of their wines he liked and all would be forgiven. He had a knack for identifying the

truly brilliant winemakers, so he would drill into their methods and that gave him more knowledge about geology and geography.

So, Philip – more than most of his peers – has been able to step outside the critic's circle and on to the battlefield. He saw as madness the vine-pull fever that swept the 1980s. How mad was it? Red grape growers got a fixed price of $186 per tonne regardless of quality. So, encouraged by a government-sponsored scheme offering $4000 an acre, they grubbed out the low yielding, old vines. The very vines that would be worth a fortune today. Priceless now: carignane, dolcetto and cinsault. What was a wine rebel to do? Dream up a plan to get the common people to understand how vital the wine industry was to the State.

Thus was born Philip's Adelaide Vine and Wine Project, commissioned by the *Advertiser* in 1989, launched by Premier John Bannon. It had two prongs. One called for a reduction in wine tax, while also giving South Australians a context for the implications for the local economy. The other prong was to provide an education in winemaking for readers already proud of living in the nation's most productive state. With a supercharged world leader called Penfolds. It sounded like a lot of fun – and it was, with citizens queuing up to be part of a winemaking exercise that went from grape to the shelf.

As much as Philip loves a frolic, he was at least equally motivated by what he saw as morally warped: the heavyweights smashing the featherweights of the industry. He launched into a state of what colleague Sly knows as 'absolute' Philip. The ulterior motive of the wine giants, Philip said, was to remove pesky individuals and small operations so they could 'deliver a homogenised, dead reliable industrial consistency of flavour with no hiccups'. Philip wrote:

In the eighties, arrogant viticulturists were still convinced that with their new science and theories of canopy management, chemicals, poisons and whatnot, their technology could always overcome the wiles of nature. That was the decade, after all, in which very big wineries quietly conspired with a naive State government to mount the notorious vine-pull scheme. On the face of it this was a noble plan to rationalise inefficient grape growers with cash incentives to pull up their vines and get out of the business. One didn't have to look very hard to realise it was really an attempt to clean out the Barossa's peasant-scale patchwork of old vineyards, limit the number of growers, and remodel the Valley's viticulture to make it more consistently, industrially samey, like Coonawarra. Starved of proper payment for their grapes, they uprooted and burnt their grandfathers' vine gardens, their Tate, Louvre, Parthenon, Guggenheim and Kew Gardens of wine heritage treasures and cried in the pubs for two years. It was a battle, but we stopped that.

No coincidence, then, that hands-on production support came from a Barossa giant, the late Peter Lehmann, who freely made the wines. 'Peter knew the Barossa was special,' Philip says. 'We got it stopped on the basis of amenity, that it would change the appearance of the Barossa too much. It was a planning issue that tripped them up.'

The *Advertiser* Vine and Wine campaign ran between 1989 and 1991. It touched a nerve, again because of concern over wanton vineyard destruction. The city was full of old vineyards dating back to the 1840s. Many houses sit on land that was once occupied by quietly superb vines. All because so many vineyards – some of them treasures – had been removed over decades.

Penfolds legend Max Schubert – a beloved friend and mentor to Philip – was upset about precious areas being ripped up at

Magill as far back as 1952. Large chunks were being sold for subdivision by Adelaide Steamship Company because the cost of running the vineyards was nearly twice that of running them elsewhere. That the Penfolds wines from Magill were the most profitable of all was ignored because of a quirk in the Steamship accounting system. Max eventually won the day, but not before damage had been done. The ripping out of vines had been going on for a long time – all the way from the foothills of Skye to the coast at Brighton. So *Advertiser* readers were bringing in some high quality grapes, related to ones originally planted by masters.

All sorts of side effects appeared, says Philip:

> One year, we raised 120 grand for homeless alcoholics. It was a shot over the bow for would-be vine pullers – some of whom were overly enthusiastic when moods changed and certain varieties went in and out of favour.

Readers got caught up in the excitement of it all. Learning to prune. Knowing what and when to spray. Arriving as early as 5 am, they'd travel from far and wide to bring their grapes to Botanic Park, where wine bins and trucks stood ready for shipping to Lehmann. Queues stretched along North Terrace to the back of the Adelaide Zoo. 'One old lady came in a taxi,' Philip says.

> She'd gone to the supermarket to buy a brown bag of grapes because she wanted to be in it. I think she made the newspaper. News of it went around the world. Old Italian blokes in Norwood wanted to buy the grapes to make their own wine.

All this was not lost on the new kid in town, Colin James, a young journalist from New Zealand.

> I was told I had to find a guy called Philip White and talk to him about the vines project. It originally was a campaign to reduce

wine tax under Section 31A. Then it also became a plan to gather unused grapes from backyards across the city so wine could be made. The purpose was to educate people about viticulture and how wine was made.

Colin tracked down Philip and, together, they found the oldest vine in the State, which was at Hamilton Estate in Marion.

> I was just blown out by the guy. Philip was larger than life; he held court in the front bar of the Exeter and I got brought into his world. He introduced me to amazing people that were just as large as him. A who's who of winemakers. Philip cares passionately, he's a true patriot of this State. Adelaide is blessed to have him as one of its characters.

Despite the resounding success of the Vine Pull campaign for both Philip and the *Advertiser*, they parted ways soon after – unceremoniously. As luck would have it, one door opened as the other one slammed. It happened at a time when a relatively new publication, the *Independent Weekly*, was looking for unique talent to build the newspaper's image.

Ever since the Adelaide daily tabloid afternoon newspaper closed in 1992, local journalists had pinned their career hopes on publications competing – in some way – with Rupert Murdoch's dominant morning daily *Advertiser*.

Paul Hamra, managing director of Solstice Media, recalls: 'Soon after we started the *Independent Weekly*, I remember getting a call from Philip in 2006 wanting to have a chat. He showed me a letter from the *Advertiser*'s Mel Mansell, dismissing him and thanking him for his years of service at NewsCorp. It was a two-paragraph letter. Philip wasn't impressed.

'He was convinced his column was dropped from the *Advertiser* because the big wine retailer s were demanding reviews on lower cost, popularist wine brands and his reviews were often about hard to find, or obscure, wines – which definitely could not be found at Liquorland.

'I knew it was an opportunity for him to keep writing but more so an opportunity for the *Independent Weekly* to secure a great Adelaide writer, with a pesky following, perfect for a paper struggling to develop an identity.

'The next thing, I was invited to his farewell party from the *Advertiser*, which was an unofficial event organised by his friends and supporters like Bob McLean, Margaret Lehmann and George Aldridge, who wanted to recognise his writing contribution to the wine industry. It was an afternoon at the Rising Sun Hotel in Gawler. Everyone was there. In his farewell speech, Whitey welcomed me to the party and announced he was joining the *Independent Weekly*.

'The following week, before his first column, I asked Philip if we should announce his arrival at the *Independent Weekly* with some PR fanfare. He said, 'Nup, they'll find me.' He was right, they did.'

David Washington has been editor of the successor publication, *InDaily*, now exclusively online, from 2012. Now managing editor, he said: 'Whitey encapsulates for me the essence of independent journalism – beholden to no-one and fiercely determined to examine the facts, no matter how uncomfortable they may be.

In our time working with him, he was never cowed by any wine industry interests, despite pressures and complaints. He was one of the few wine writers with a regular gig who would bite the hand that feeds – not because he wanted to be provocative for the sake of it, but because he cares deeply, not just about wine, but about the country.

Beyond the sometimes difficult themes he writes about, he's also challenging to editors because of his unconventional use of language – something that became more remarkable in the latter part of his time with *InDaily*. He developed a language that was all his own but remained comprehensible to regular readers, even if it made you stop and think for a while. His use of metaphors breaks convention. It's not surprising that Whitey loves poetry and has serious talent as a poet.

When Whitey told me he was ill, it was devastating, but he carried himself with dignity, gratitude and, in his personal messages, that distinctive sense of poetry. I imagined, then, that his capacity to describe things with such specificity, such clarity, could be a comfort to him – I hope I'm right.

Whitey has had an impact on every Australian wine writer who cares about the vocation as a craft. Like every great writer in any subject, Whitey's words have always been about more than the subject at hand - they're about the whole messy, confusing and beautiful enterprise that is life.

Award-winning journalist Hendrik Gout was editor of the Adelaide independent newspaper between 2006 and 2010. He believes Philip was so readable that even teetotallers were able to get a kick out of his wide-ranging wine columns.

'Just as some of the best travel stories – or restaurant reviews – can be enjoyed by people who are never going to go to these places or dine in them, so it was with Philip's columns. He always kept to deadlines, which is critical.'

CHAPTER 25

If Phar Lap is *the* Australian Horse, then Penfolds ...

'Peter really found his feet in 1990 when Ross Wilson took over the helm as managing director . . . Ross was the first who said we've got to stop this secrecy, talk to people and be honest about what we do.' – Philip White

Peter Gago knows he lives in a comfortable bubble called Penfolds. He got one of his 'rude awakenings' in Beverly Hills on an umpteenth working tour of the US. Watching a fire burning four kilometres away, threatening to swallow the Getty Museum. It didn't take him long to think of home, and what could happen to the silken treasures cellared at Magill, including Australia's most sought-after and established series, Grange. If Phar Lap is our horse, Grange is our wine. And according to Milton Wordley's blog winetenquestions.com.au, Gago has been known to assert wine is 'up there Cazaly' with sport in the eyes of contemporary Aussies.

On paper, it looks so easy. The transition from departed chief winemaker John Duval to the more-than-promising maths and science teacher who, despite rapid promotions, had switched careers to carve a name for himself in champagne. Even today, Gago can't come up with a snappy explanation for how he got the job that led to being Penfolds' chief winemaker, arguably the most prestigious in all the land. Humility perhaps. Work ethic? What does stick in his mind was the strict hierarchy governing workers at wineries in the seventies and early eighties. Not quite *Downtown Abbey*, but close.

> You'd never call David Wynn 'David'. It was Mister Wynn – there was a very ritualistic structure. You would almost take your hat off if you wore one. And many did in the day.

A far cry from the individualistic exuberance of a few twenty-first-century barons, who have, in turn, replaced the serious blokes in R.M. Williams moleskins and Range Rovers.

One of the concomitants of the post, it would seem, is dealing with Philip, who was close to both indispensable Grange pioneers, wine chemist Dr Ray Beckwith and Max Schubert. The 'brash young punk wine writer' loved and admired both men to the point of devotion. But what sets him apart from many peers is that he might have been a handful, but he actually listened hard to the words of the older men.

Philip White enjoys replaying the tale of former stablehand Schubert, 'a lovely, quiet, respectful man who lived in a cellar at Magill', and the way he kept it secret from his employers that he was working away on an unheard of wine called Grange, in the 1950s.

> Max just opened his door to me and taught me everything. He never withheld a secret from me. He had secrets from his employers. It's a classic piece of Australian industrial psychology forelock tugging versus foresight in a way. While the family-run Penfolds sent Max to Spain to study sherry, he ended up in Bordeaux. On the flight home, Max was already plotting the wine regarded as our greatest, most significant. And he had to do it with cheaper oak than he wanted, that is American oak rather than French oak, and a cheaper grape – shiraz rather than cabernet.

Why did this young whippersnapper listen to a much older man? 'He had style.' Right then, a look of purest joy crosses Philip's face.

> He was a really stylish man with a good brain and he was honest. Max used to say: 'Wine's got to have soul. Got be like your mum, motherly and comforting.' And, like me, he grew up in a village. I grew up opposite a blacksmith. His dad was the blacksmith. I knew what his home smelled like when he was a boy. Like soot and the old man's sweaty apron and then jam and cakes, strudel, you know, beautiful things.

In Philip's opinion, Gago wears Schubert's heavy crown comfortably, despite a gruelling spin-round-the-world travel schedule.

> I can't believe how he does it. He can't sleep on planes because he lives on them. And I don't know anyone in the whole wine industry who raises more millions for his company than Peter. Peter's Granges are as good as Max's. Some of them. He had to upgrade it from a very right-wing, over-oaked, American naked wine to something that's more suited to the current climate in the wine business. Make it a more elegant wine in a way. Without destroying its image, losing its clientele; very hard to do.

Peter really found his feet in 1990 when Ross Wilson took over the helm as managing director, having paid AUD$410 million for Penfolds and a collection of other top wine brands from the billion-dollar wreckage of failed conglomerate Adsteam. 'Ross was the first who said we've got to stop this secrecy, talk to people and be honest about what we do,' Philip says.

> It was absentee landlords to start with; management was in Sydney. They didn't know anything about winemaking or marketing, which let Max develop Grange in the first place. Very few critics have ever attacked Grange. There are a lot of young journalists who like attacking it, to make their name, but it's like attacking the Vatican. Mark Shields came out against one

> vintage, 'strange Grange' I remember he called it. That really stuck on it. It was probably a slight change of style.
>
> I've criticised its oak, I didn't like the big American oaky ones they're selling – but who am I? I have been really critical of it over the years. It just got too big and woody and brash. Too obvious, it lacked finesse, you needed to keep it for thirty-five years. Peter's been a very good friend in the sense that he accepted my criticism and my praise of his efforts.

Gago revels in the rich history. 'We're 175 years, it's our anniversary year,' he says. 'It's a very traditional house, but also innovative.' He says Philip is something of an anarchist at heart, but one of his contradictory characteristics is his huge respect for history and knowledge.

> Look at his relationship with Dr Ray Beckwith, who died a few weeks short of his 101st birthday. He was doing things with wine before anybody else in Italy, France, Germany, anywhere. The Cambridge PH electronic meter was used for the first time on planet Earth behind closed doors at the secretive family-owned Penfolds. [And it led to the finding that controlling acidity could limit bacterial growth and reduce spoilage from high to practically zero, saving a fortune.]
>
> For someone who'd be on a very fine wire between anarchy and whatever, Philip was correct in his history, he didn't rewrite it. Penfolds are indebted to his insight and his acknowledgement of Dr Beckwith. Philip was into active listening, as modern-day managers would call it. A lot of people said of Paul Keating as a younger man, a fledgling politician, he used to spend a lot of time with the tribal elders in the ALP. He said, in an interview with the elderly and the old and the wise we get all this information distilled. Philip in his wisdom was very much like that too. With the older wine characters, he's getting condensed history and a better overview from those people.

It's been long acknowledged he's the finest wine writer in Australia. But always qualified in inverted commas, 'when in form'. Can be, but not always. I know a lot of overseas wine writers used him as a bit of a gatekeeper on their trips to South Australia when it was much more difficult to get here. They found twenty minutes with Philip was worth four hours on the phone to winemakers. The gatekeeper role is the ultimate endorsement from your peers.

Gago admires Philip's honesty, intellect and big picture awareness.

The connectivity – some people look at things in isolation, but he's able to put a lot of different things together. Philip has talked up so many great Australian wines and he's torn down pretenders too. He's very good at separation of Church and State.

Honesty is his biggest weapon but also is his biggest scourge and he walks a fine line. As easily as he can create great and lifelong friendships, he can disenfranchise people as well. It's not a chameleonic thing, it's the honesty, the integrity, the intellect all put together and he's his own worst enemy in that regard. I've heard him dress down people before and it can be quite brutal. I'm not saying these people shouldn't have been dressed down, but there are many ways to do it without really offending. I've got an educational background so I've had to use peer-group pressure to work on class bullies, on loudmouths. In eight-and-a-half years of teaching, I never raised my voice once. I used other tools, but they didn't include humiliation.

I'm not suggesting that Philip ever has – intentionally. It's not a lack of sensitivity, he is very sensitive, so I suspect he'd oftentimes wake up the next morning and think did I really say that? We know the history with his parents and everything else. He can give a great speech, he can give a great talk, go straight

> to the bone, use emotion, honesty, all part of the repertoire of a preacher.
>
> He's a very complex human being. A likeable rogue, but a rogue nevertheless. When you use the term larrikin, it has a perception of nice and happy but I think there is a dark side to Philip. In his earlier stronger days, he acted very much like the Viking he imagined being. In terms of women and drink and the naughty sort of behaviour in a very manly way. Now he lacks testosterone [due to cancer treatment]. A lot of what he thought and feared and didn't understand is now perhaps making more sense, seeing the other side, so to speak. He's panned some of our wines quite brutally, given our penchant for American oak. There have been very amusing negative comments about our wine.

In any event, the two men clearly see each other through a prism of affection and high regard. 'I look forward to one day soon exchanging true banter in the old Philip style,' says Gago. He is well aware of the task ahead.

> People say Penfolds is a strong brand – brands live and die by the sword. They can fall by the wayside overnight. One scandal, one bit of arrogance, can lead to a chain of events and there goes your brand. A lot of people, including ones who run this country, say what Australia needs is a luxury brand and Penfolds is ideally poised. I'd love Penfolds to be a luxury brand but we're not. The French do it so well, why can't an Australian brand do it? I say the difference is they live, breathe, sweat everything 24/7. Luxury is not a light switch you switch on and off. I would love Penfolds to do it but we're not there yet.
>
> That includes the way the Chinese see us, too. The crucial attraction there is the coincidence of design, which suits the Oriental penchant for lucky numbers. The luck is as follows:

> A red capsule – they love red, the red stamp. The use of Bin numbers they can relate to the number 8. In Mandarin the name is pronounced almost 'Benfolds', and who'd believe it means Route to Prosperity?

Gago is full of praise for Philip's contribution to the internationally released book, *A Day in the Life of Grange*, by photographer Milton Wordley. Philip writes of his many glasses of wine with Schubert and Beckwith.

> In that home stretch of their lives that I witnessed, they shared an old-fashioned combination of confident pride and quiet humility. Like Ray, Max had a child-like trust in the acuity and persistence of his curiosity. Both men had deep faith in their ability to question the status quo, the state of the art. They were improvers, always testing their brains for better ways of doing things.
>
> Peter Gago has become another treasured friend and wise mentor in this very different age. Grange is secure with Peter and his stalwart team . . . a curious generation: a school of winemakers of rare gastronomic intelligence who show unflinching respect for their vinous inheritance, but combine this with an untiring, continual review of how and why things are done, always pestering their own science and art for better ideas.

Friends maybe . . . however, Philip admits he can be 'scared to talk' to the maker of such hallowed wine; daren't ask questions, lest Peter feel the need to respond at the risk of annoying his masters.

> I know he's spent an incredible amount of his time protecting his brands from the owners. He'll probably hate me saying this, but I will. Guess who makes the most money for the company?

> Peter put together 3G, a beautiful blend of three Granges at $3000 each. Sold out in thirty-six hours. They [managements] force their creative minds to do things they know wouldn't be approved. In a sense, they've put him in a position a bit like Max (Schubert) was in, and we all know he had to keep secrets from the bosses.

It is well known Philip upsets winemakers, big and small. An example arose in a 2018 interview with a weekly podcast, *The Adelaide Show*, which celebrates all things good about South Australia. According to the interviewer, the winemaker, Philip Shaw was asked how he felt about their wine writer guest. Shaw grunted before replying: 'That arse-hat. I respect him for all his knowledge. But when we were winning awards at bushing festivals, he didn't lift his gaze or give us credit where it was due.'

Philip later said he had known Shaw since his early days, and he was the Golden Boy for Rosemount, which, in a 'white knight' act, had taken over Penfolds from the ailing Southcorp in what was initially described as a merger. Philip said he had eagerly awaited Shaw's first release in the refreshed Penfolds Bin line.

Philip publicly expressed disappointment in the latest offering, adding:

> A couple of hours later, Shaw phones me and says it had not been his intention to release wines like that, and that he was withdrawing the entire line. They released a much superior wine. I said as much at the time – I've actually been very good to Rosemount when they do the right thing.

CHAPTER 26

Not R U OK? You Are OK!

'Philip gave me that notion that who you are is OK and you're a decent sort of person . . . when I was terrified of being the person I thought I was.' – George Grainger Aldridge, artist

Artist George Grainger Aldridge is one of those people you can place in a modestly exalted position. Easygoing. Gentle minded. An acclaimed popular painter and cartoonist with a whimsical outlook. Can't change the world, but can make people laugh at its absurdities. Safe to say he has a good name and reputation around the universe, including with folks like actor Arnie Schwarzenegger, with whom he exchanges drawings and messages. The Aldridge name in South Australia goes back to the mid-1800s. 'The other connection is my father's aunt, Rose Grainger, Percy Grainger's mother. Percy was my godfather and great-uncle. I did get to meet Ella, Percy's wife. That was back in the sixties. She was a vegan.'

That Aldridge and Philip White are great mates is no surprise when you get to know them both. They have the outward soft open faces of true monks. And the inner steel of a true monk. Then there is the Exeter connection. At the Rundle Street corner of the front bar, with its ambience of an old country town bric-a-brac shop, owner Kevin Gregg has given pride of place to Aldridge's work. One of the big beauties that used to hang there was whisked off to Singapore via London. An Adelaide IT guru who now lives in the UK saw *Flinders Granges*, a painting based on the dreamy landscape of the Flinders Ranges on the edge of the South Australian desert, about 425 kilometres north of Adelaide, and had to have it. Knew it would suit a good friend in Singapore, as it combined two favourites. Aldridge had playfully placed – among stunningly rendered red rocks and spinifex near Wilpena Pound – cartoonish bottles of Penfolds Grange, one of the most expensive and sought-after wines of South Australia.

'It takes that mystery-cum-elitism out of the wine,' the creator reckons.

> It pays homage but looks at it in a natural, Aussie way. Bloke that bought it, he and his mate often crack open a bottle of Grange when they get together. I was wandering up the footpath to the Exeter and Kevin goes, 'This is the bloke here, the painter.' The bloke says: 'Name your price.'
>
> Bang. That's the thing about the Exeter, it's got the most eclectic group of people – better than any gallery. You've got a captive audience, lots of grog and they buy the stuff. No commission. The last one was again a buyer from London, a painting of a galah. Michael, a money mover. Now he's commissioned me to do a painting of the Exeter. Also the man who runs Olympic Industries, he's a fan.

That front bar area is Aldridge's wall of fame and fortune, though he insists both are small. Fans of his might be surprised to hear just how modest are his means, as he flits between stays at Blinman and his spartan, zero-running-water warehouse studio in Kent Town. Put it this way, the sighs of simple pleasure coming from inside whichever home Aldridge is babysitting at the time can be heard all around the neighbourhood. Like the good bushman he is, Aldridge can turn his touch to many things for a few dollars more. Perhaps helping out shearers or coaching the footy club. One of his long-term business associations is with the Northern Cattleman's Association in the NT.

> They know how to use cartoons in a serious industry staring down the determined face of the animal rights' movement. One of the first cartoons I did was this thin, gaunt, emaciated character with a shield – Conan the Vegetarian. It's become their major image.

So it comes as a jolt to hear George tell of his doubts about himself, his low self-esteem. 'I always felt isolated because of who I thought I was,' George says. Before he bumped into Philip. He's not the first person to point to Philip as someone who offers unconditional encouragement. An amateur mentor.

> Philip gave me the notion that who you are is OK and you're a decent sort of person. It was lovely to hear somebody say that about me when I was terrified of being the person I thought I was. He gave me a new person to actually carry with me. This was when I first met him. Also, seeing Philip in action was to believe it was a good place to be. He was a pretty outrageous character, and I could never be that, but he took me to the next level, and I never thought I'd get there. He made me feel good about it. Confident. That the work I was doing was worthwhile. To think that I got that recognition, not from standing in front of a huge crowd at an exhibition but by talking with Philip.
>
> I remember some artwork I did when I was in Venice. A big long drawing that goes out over a metre. He was there when I first got off the plane. He said: 'Fuck, that is just beautiful.' That meant so much to me. From then, I just went, no, what I'm doing is OK. It's not like I needed his recognition all the time. But he put me in a place that what I was doing was worthwhile.

Within the realms of the art world, as a painter, you don't get much recognition. Not that you ask for it, but occasionally it's a prerequisite for keeping you upright and doing what you do. Eking out some pathetic existence. Because I knew he was doing the same. He talked about his work in the same way as he talked about mine. He brought out that other person in me, a bit of respect for yourself is OK. It was joyous – still is. He was always intensely interested in what I was doing, and with great integrity. I've never said that to him. It's a natural part of him. He's not forcing himself, that's the lovely thing about it.

This is another dimension of him as a person. It's like discovering a new element in the field of geology. He adds another element to human life. I've never met anybody like him. And probably never will. The alien spacecraft had probably just left [chuckles] – Philip waving to it and saying to them: 'I'll be back in a while.'

Countless are the tales of fun and derring-do on journeys involving Philip. Usually involving swigs from an ever-present bottle of whisky, with a vast array of mates and freshly unwrapped acquaintances. One day, George and Philip were tootling back to Adelaide. They'd been at a cookout at Blinman in the Flinders Ranges. As they passed an engineering company called Mid-North Fabricators, Philip yelled out, 'Great name for a newspaper!' leaving them both laughing about the twist on Trump's fake news for the next twenty kays. On a good day, Philip had a facility for putting strangers at ease. The local copper pulled the two men over. Philip promptly handed him the whisky and told him to have a swig. Two days later, George spotted them enjoying whiskies at the Blinman Hotel.

George, like Philip, has never owned a television. He observes Philip amasses an astonishing amount of information nonetheless.

'He's like a human version of Google,' George says. On road trips, Philip could talk as much about the fence posts as about the geography or the geology. What would appear to most of us as mundane scenery would ignite Philip into a zone of beautiful, rolling conversation. George does his best to illustrate: 'That strata there will reappear somewhere else.' Or: 'There's a natural spring that runs along here.'

> He knows things in great detail. Every aspect of the land you're on. All while drinking from a bottle of whisky. Still maintaining his incredible focus. The way he serves that knowledge is remarkable. A bucket load of information pours out. It's not about ego, he's not showing off. It's complex but it's not about complexity. It's about putting that information out in a way that's really digestible.
>
> I go to see Philip and I'm prepared not for a lesson but a journey. He takes you for a wander and that's the great joy. He makes the world of information so sumptuous. I keep saying to people, 'Philip is one of the most remarkable thinkers.'
>
> When I was up in Kanmantoo, wandering around with him there, he's literally picking up dirt and tasting the soil. He knew what he was wanting to taste. He once described a wine to me, the smell – and I don't have an acute sense of smell. But he described the wine as 'old school ruler'. It was perfect. That took me back thirty years to primary school. It brings you to a screaming halt, the way he puts things. The other was 'the smell of a wet dog'.

It is not hard to find people who find Philip less likeable than the portrait painted by George. And even those who get past that renowned Philip barbed-wire fence to a closer position were usually scared of him at first sight. Philip describes his keep-away punk demeanour as a necessary carapace to discourage the unwanted, boring or bothersome. George:

> In the beginning I had an enormous fear of him. Yet now I feel nothing but a great love and affection for him. He takes me where I've never been before; he has this intriguing accuracy and detail about the ground he stands on. I love listening to him. He's taught me how to be a good listener. He gives information so freely and easily and generously. Driving with him is a delight. He moves across the planet and civilisation with such wonderful insight.

But like a brother, George has seen the other side of Philip, and can handle the contrast without rancour.

> I've seen him snap and lose his temper, be bewilderingly scary, like a volcano. One time, I couldn't understand it, seemed like for no apparent reason. Somebody had said or done something which annoyed him and he just blew.
>
> Wow, I thought, I must watch where these triggers are because I don't want to be on the receiving end of it [laughs]. And yet I never have been. He's always treated me with a great deal of respect and love. I grew more comfortable with him, but that took a while.

George takes a moment to consider how he would go about depicting Philip's volatility. 'Lots of colour,' he says, smiling.

> Like a massive fireworks display. Interesting to look at but make sure you're not in close proximity. The people on the wrong end are in total shock. And yet I've seen him with people, and he's just the softest, most gentle caring man. He can be brittle and harsh and scary, yet there's this other side of him glowing with love and care. The other thing I find outstanding is his respect for people he feels deserve it. He observes people very closely and gleans a great deal of detail. He's doesn't waffle over people,

> his scrutiny is very intense. He maintains an enormous amount of integrity in the way he approaches people, which I don't see in many others.

George, from a photo, did a painting of Philip's beloved mother Sylvia. Philip was overcome with emotion at her memory, one shared with many people who saw her as exceptionally soft and kind. Just as some onlookers see Philip as a serial womaniser, a walk-in-walk-out lover of brittle loyalty, others know him differently. Ex-lovers with more than one axe to grind highlight a tender, fun-loving, unpredictable, romantic and thoughtful side rarely glimpsed in others. A remarkable number of women are still madly in love with Philip, albeit from a wide variety of geographical and other distances.

Journalist Colin James scrolls down his mobile phone to show me a photo of a very attractive woman who used to go out with Philip. Now living interstate, she jumped on a plane when she heard about the cancer. 'She's still in love with him,' James says.

> Look at the admiration in her eyes. Women find him incredibly attractive. They hit on him. They can see the poet. The vision. The fineness of the man. I think he'd be quite an adventurous lover. A lot of women would have enjoyed being in his bed.
>
> I think he'd be a giver, not a taker. He's had some beautiful women in his life. Sometimes he's broken their hearts and sometimes they've broken his heart and that can hit him hard.

Philip has often cared very deeply about the women in his life, to the extent that break-ups have sent him into a black, downward spiral for weeks on end. George:

> I've seen Philip at his highest peaks and I've seen him crash. The crashes come hard, too. I can see that through his poetry, a lot of his writing, illustrations. That internalising of the anguish that

> comes through. I've seen him in various love relationships where there's been incredible trauma and anguish. I've had to rescue him a few times. Drive halfway across the State to put him into a safe place. I've seen him in quite disturbing relationships of great intensity; I've had to go in and bail him out.

There is a great affinity between George the artist and Philip, the young man who saw himself becoming a painter towards the end of his days. George is able to describe the teacher, the life whisperer that many meet but cannot quite explain. 'Philip walks and talks with you,' he says.

> It's not simply giving information. I asked him about wine barrels the other day and suddenly I felt like I was inside a barrel. The lovely way he described it all as he talked me through the science of wine barrels. At the end of it, I could taste that wine coming out of that barrel. He's got you by the hand and you're doing the same journey with him. You're talking and walking, smelling and tasting with him. He's not just handing it to you and expecting you're going to understand it, when he talks about the dirt and the soil and what formation that is.
>
> I remember we were coming round the corner by the Salopian Hotel and there was this big vineyard. He said, 'They shouldn't have planted vines there. That's Bay of Biscay soil, when it dries out, it's crap. Doesn't hold moisture very well at all.' I drove by a week later and they'd taken all the vines out.

George himself is a man whose knowledge and empathy have not gone unnoticed, however modest he may be. George's son Jack is a chef and wanted a birthday card from the star of films like *The Terminator*. George knew how to get Arnie's attention without getting flamed. He had heard about Arnie's fondness for R.M. Williams' clothes and boots, which led him to occasionally sneak into Australia. So, when he was governor of California,

George sent him an apt cartoon featuring the outback outfitter. Not long afterwards, a birthday card arrived for Jack – 'from your old mate, Arnie' – and a set of gold cufflinks. 'Arnie has three or four pieces of my work,' George says. 'He's this most gentle, lovely man, totally different to his image.'

George's special talents have also been in demand from our Indigenous tribes. He now fondly recalls a very tense few minutes with visitors to the SA Museum, where he was an artist and designer. He made drawings of sacred objects because photos were forbidden by Aboriginals. 'They see something quite false in photographs,' George says. One day, he found himself in the museum's sacred room on North Terrace. Slowly, the atmosphere stiffened. One by one, a group of tribal Elders entered. Silently, they formed a circle, walking around George. Looking at him. Inspecting. Not in a particularly warm and friendly fashion. Darting glances. Suspicion. Nary a word spoken. 'It still gives me goosebumps when I think of it,' George says.

> I was told in no uncertain terms that I was never to divulge the nature of the sacred items. They've stood around me in a circle for a number of minutes and then said: 'No, no, he's okay.' They were sensing who I was, was I the right person for the task. It was a great honour. I was very conscious of the fact I was dealing with very sacred objects that weren't to be seen by anybody else. The Elders would decide where those sacred objects would go to be reinstalled in their sites.

Philip often makes George laugh out loud. 'One of the specialists treating Philip's cancer at Flinders Medical Centre told him he'd give him five extra years of life – a huge bonus given the patient was expected to die early in 2019. Quick as a flash, Philip replied, "I don't think I can afford that."'

CHAPTER 27

Can Taste in Colours, Can't See Green

'No longer did he see it as an affliction, it was a gift.'
– Leon Bignell in reference to Philip having synaesthesia

One way to explain Philip's ability to blend doses of good luck and bad luck into a nourishing, serendipitous drink is to observe the day not long ago he burst into tears and kept crying for an hour. He was sitting on the front verandah of his rented cottage surrounded by Yangarra vineyards, feasting his eyes on a sumptuous, mouth-watering rainbow view you could eat over a very long lunch. One that Philip himself had seen in a way only understood by the colour deficient. They usually lack access to green, which means the difference between colours turns varying degrees of muddy, though not completely monochromatic, as there is access to blue and red.

News of a tool that could help came via the brains trust at Flinders Medical Centre, via surgeons who had used EnChroma colour blind glasses for operations. These provide more contrast between the different waves of light, according to Dr Ivan Schwab of the American Academy of Ophthalmology. They make it easier for the brain to differentiate medium wavelengths from long ones. However, while EnChroma products make a difference, they are not an actual cure for colour blindness. The colour story doesn't end there.

Leon 'Biggles' Bignell put it this way:

> Philip has synaesthesia, this rare condition where he tastes everything in colour. Same with Van Gogh. As a kid, Philip didn't understand it, it was something that set him apart and he thought he was a bit of a loser because he had it and he used to behave in a certain way to cover up what he thought was a disability. It was once he got into writing about wine and the link between geology and the terroir and the wines, he could just see it so clearly. He was receiving those glowing reports back, so that no longer did he see it as an affliction, it was a gift and that was a big turning point in his life in terms of confidence.

The EnChroma glasses, made in California, don't come cheap. But Philip's ability to attract patrons came into its own. He was having a drink at the Salopian Inn one day when he bumped into an old friend. 'John Dodd the stockbroker gave me two grand towards the glasses,' Philip explains.

> I hadn't seen him in ten or fifteen years and he came to my table and said: 'I've heard what's going on [with your cancer], send me your bank account details and I'll send you some money. I give money away every Christmas. I'd prefer to give it to you.' Which helped me get these miraculous shades. When Albert Bensimon heard about the colour blindness shades because I asked him if he, being a jeweller, could import them, he dove down and gave me another two grand. It was out of competition between him and John. Albert wouldn't have given me that money if he hadn't heard of Johnny giving me the two grand in that restaurant. I know what happened.

It is a well-known – if mildly puzzling – fact that Philip attracts wealthy benefactors who will simply and willingly hand him large amounts of cash. Their reward is to be allowed access, an all-areas backstage pass, to his front bar and other performances. Bensimon is a classic example of this twenty-first-century version of patronage of the arts. While it is fuelled by generosity, Gus Howard sees the gifts as something less romantic. 'That's called purchasing love,' he argues.

> Don't make any mistake about it. That's a person who is an achiever and successful but he doesn't really know how to be himself. He doesn't believe he can be accepted for himself. Philip attracts those kinds of people and he has to be very careful about how he manages them. Because he makes it look so easy, and the fact that he doesn't seek fortune from it makes it all the more alluring.

CHAPTER 28
Men of Category

'He's had an outstanding life. That's what he's got to show for it all.' – Leon Bignell

Philip has always walked the same dead-straight line when it comes to Mammon. The greedy pursuit of material wealth is not his bag. His attitude is made clear in a speech he made to the SA Wine Press Club at the Exeter Hotel on 27 March 2002.

> I want to read to you the opening passage from 'One Man's Ambition', the introduction to Wynn Winegrowers Diary, 1970, written by the late Walter James, who was a great and humble wine writer in Melbourne. When you choose to direct your life to the task of making money you may be sure that your success will arouse the admiration, and the envy, of a vast army of men who have had similar aims. Should you set out not to make money but to make something really worthwhile in itself, your success will with equal certainty be rewarded with the admiration, and the goodwill, of men who really matter – men of category, as the Spaniards call them.
>
> In some fields of productive endeavour, of course, you cannot achieve much without substantial means; it is only a little sad that so many men of ability as they reach for success and meet it are beguiled into allowing the means to submerge the aim and in the end are content to do, adequately enough, no more than a hundred others around them are doing equally well. Their

obituaries describe these people as successful businessmen and they pass promptly into oblivion.

On the other hand, there is a side to Philip that is highly receptive to a dollar or a thousand. 'I love having money and there have been times in my life when I've had quite a lot of it,' he says.

> I've had odd jobs that have worked out all right, windfall jobs in mining. When I was in mining I was earning a lot of money. Four-hundred-dollar Italian shoes. Morellis [gurgles a laugh]. Cath fell for me because of the shoes.

While all that is true, it is also well documented that Philip had a strong sense of thought-out purpose that led him to ignore blandishments or the lure of dollars. A clue to his – at times – wilful blindness to opportunities for growing wealth may lie in a childhood chore: circulating the collection plate for his preacher father Jimmy. Philip tackles the issue in a passage from his drinkster.com blog.

> As the eldest son, I was skilled at observing exactly how much money each constituent put in the plate as I did the collection after they'd drunk Jesus' blood but before the preaching. When they hid their contribution in an envelope, I was expert at remembering which was theirs. Dad never asked the details; I never confessed. But I learned a lot about tithing. And I've never really understood or wanted money since.

Max Allen, drinks writer for the *Australian Financial Review*, has long been painfully aware of how hard it is for anybody to get rich in the game. In 2015, he told online wine business magazine *WBM*:

> Unless you've already established a brand through print, like Jancis Robinson and Robert Parker have done, and your brand is

> desirable enough for people to pay for it, there's no future for it. Philip is a classic example; drinkster.com – I reckon that's one of the best wine blogs out there, and there's room for intelligent, erudite, articulate opinions like Philip's, but how's he making a living out of that? For those of us who've still got kids at home, bills to pay, mortgages to pay off, it's a bit of a worry really.

Music provides a classic example of Philip's penchant for choosing love over money. He has long been obsessed with music, as a fan and a guitar player. Asked whether he took music as far as he'd have liked, Philip said:

> I think I did the right thing. Not monetarily or business-wise but for my own satisfaction. I could have been a cinematographer, a journalist or a musician. Writing was a smart move.

Though Philip's attitude could be seen as laudable in the fast-repeating ages of Greed Is Good, it is also exasperating. Just ask Albert Bensimon. In vain, the jeweller has tried to instruct the wordsmith as to how to make more money without compromising his firm beliefs. Journalist Colin James agrees that money has rarely, if ever, been a prime motivation for Philip. 'He's scratched it. It takes balls to choose that way of life. There have been many crises in Philip's life with money.'

According to good friend George Grainger Aldridge, Philip's fierce independence has cost him dearly.

> The acquisition of wealth doesn't seem to fit into Philip's equation at all. He's not going to kowtow to anybody. He's got such incredible passion for what he does, how he thinks, how he writes. How he perceives a piece of artwork or local geology. His pay, income, is the incredible knowledge he gathers. It's his currency. Artists tend to live off the smell of an oily rag – my

> wealth is in my work, whatever appears on paper. It's a horrible road at times.

George's forensic yet sensitive assessment: 'Out of his home life and background comes this extraordinary person.'

It is hazardous to calculate the impact of what we, as children, observe at home. But, given Philip's unorthodox attitude to money, it is interesting to note his retelling of how his family left Victoria for South Australia.

Pastor Jimmy gave away his worldly goods in exchange for cash and a new car and drove the family to Kanmantoo. The 1950s were boom times for the economy, in general. But, in some cases, there was a silent going-without among parents sacrificing a meal or a coat for their offspring. Unless you've grown up in a family with parents who really do run out of money for days at a time, it is not easy to understand how that affects the children, psychologically. Philip says people looked down on his family because 'we shot rabbits and ate them'.

'Mum and Dad warned us not to talk about the rabbits, not to boast.'

Recording engineer Mick Wordley understands Philip, because of his own father. Dick Wordley made a big name for himself as an investigative journalist, including with newspapers the Adelaide *News* and Melbourne *Truth*. His speciality was international child abduction, including reportage that led to his 1973 book *A Piece of Paper* on a controversial case involving a Sydney-based Greek woman and her daughter. The book inspired the award-winning *Cathy's Child*, a 1979 film featuring Michele Fawdon and Bryan Brown, with Alan Cassell as Dick. Mick:

> For all his stories and successes, my father was on a pension in the end. He could have been a wealthy man. The media always

took advantage of him, paid him a pittance, if at all. Philip is similar in that he doesn't have a lot of money but manages to get enough together to survive. Through the journey of humanity, there's always someone who's an enigma, who doesn't operate to our currencies. We worry about money but he doesn't.

Mick chuckles at the memory of his first encounter with Philip, at a Norwood hotel. Mick was playing with his R&B trio The Donkeys, which many years later performed at a benefit concert for the wine writer.

He was lying on the floor by the foot rail on the bar, pretty liquid, commenting: 'It sounds better down here. What a band!' My brother Milton said, 'Aw, that's Philip.' He turned up at all our gigs. One small thing I really liked about Philip is he'd announce: 'I'm really drunk.' Not too many people do that. They usually try to hide it. He can get a bit vicious, but that's when he comes across someone he doesn't like or has the demeanour to take him on. I've seen him take on some of my friends and it's been a bit embarrassing. That's how he sees it.

He'd probably be the most honest person in dialogue I've ever met. He's straight up and down. I can think of a couple of friends who were highly offended, and so was he. It was over an issue of opinion about a politician or something. He always gives you his full attention. He's not like a lot of people, looking over your shoulder all the time. Philip gives you his focused attention and endeavour; my wife Robyn brought that to my attention. When he came to my birthday party I was really touched, because he was crook; had a Santa Claus sack of medical equipment and drugs he had to be taking.

He has wronged a few women and my wife Robyn loves him dearly but she can also see she wouldn't want to go near him with a barge pole as far as a relationship goes because he can be a real bastard. I know a couple of ladies who had a terrible

> time with him. But they still would lay down their coat in the gutter for him. You hear him speak to them and he's so eloquent and poetic. He is who he is and won't compromise or play any pantomime.

Mick was with Philip at the funeral of his father, Pastor Jimmy, and took the haunting photo of the eldest son hunched over the grave in a shape that did not embody much grieving.

> Philip was his normal self, solemn yet jovial. He didn't sort of fall off his galloping horse. It was a day that was nice to be just all together.
>
> Philip treats his family – his brothers and sisters – with a huge respect. So I learned a lot about his family at the hall in Strathalbyn, where all the kids are running outside, there were scones and pots of tea and Philip had his whisky in his pocket.

Gus Howard:

> He doesn't like to be beholden to people, because it impacts on his freedom. Even before he had a subject [wine], he was the kind of person who reserved the right to say what he feels. You don't want to charge for that, you just want to say it. It's just possible one of the things he learned as a child was that the truth is there to be spoken. His father was supported as clergy sometimes are, but not particularly well. That's just possibly one of the ethics – for want of a better word – that he has retained from his upbringing. Selling yourself comes with some compromises. And he was never a true freelancer. In other words, he wouldn't do a job for just anyone who called him up. And that's his right, a right he's retained.

Someone who got a close-up of Philip's fiscal convolutions was 'Nadine', who had a relationship with him in the 1980s when there was wide acclaim for his courage. When he would go after the irrigators on the River Murray, and winemakers who secretly added sugar. The ex-lover says he could afford to take a stand because he had been careful never to accumulate assets that could be lost in a legal stoush.

> That was a conscious decision – he's a smart guy. I remember him saying that to me: 'I don't want to have money. Because it only creates problems. And I don't want to have anything to lose' – or words to that effect.

Another factor in the fiscal stakes is Philip's willingness to sacrifice comfort and convenience, no matter the pain. A good example is letting his driver's licence expire in 1989.

> One: 'I knew I was a danger.'
> Two: 'Buried too many young friends from traffic accidents.'
> Three: 'Breathalysers were starting to really come in.'

As has been the case in Philip's world, the thinking was angular.

> If I was half-pissed, I would sleep on the couch. But if I was full sheets, I'd drive home the back way. At 180 kilometres an hour. When I decided I was going to change my life and not drive anymore I had already moved from the Barossa to Hurtle Square in the city and I was working for the '*Tiser* so I could walk everywhere; didn't need a car.

On drinskter.com, Philip wrote, in September 2016:

> It's nearly thirty years since the writer sat at his table in the city with a bag of university tobacco and a bottle of Highland Park, watching his driver's licence expire. As a risk-taking petrol-headed booze artist who found it infernally difficult to frame his will to the law, that damn ticket to ride was a threat to society and life in general. Better remove it from himself than end up

enduring the ignominy of being lectured by the fuzz and a stern judge pointing gimlet eyes over the half-frames to deliver the ceremonial removal-as-punishment business.

No copper or wig man was gonna take that dude's licence away. I write about that dude, that dudenkopf, from a vast distance now: in many ways he was not me. We change with the sliding time. But having buried too many mates who were victims of the road, and very narrowly missing being buried himself on too many occasions, it was time to stop. Before the frothing mad Whitey killed somebody else. Showing the sort of responsibility it took to punish oneself with a lifetime grounding was most unlike that unruly young 'un with his love for speed and the thrill of risk.

But the fact was simple. A person who spent most of each working day with his nose in a snifter, or a thousand of them, could rarely boast of a blood alcohol level that fit responsible driving, whether he spat or not.

For my first decade without personal wheels, I lived in the city. That was a breeze. A free bus would collect me from my door and take me to the Central Market. There were eateries everywhere and if the pub I lived in was not enough to quench the recreational – as opposed to professional – thirst, there were six more thirst emporiums within a short swagger.

When I lived in a more conventional apartment, the fledgling Adelaide Independent Taxis were always on hand, and I found a most expert and rapid driver name of Tom Koutsantonis who quickly learned my patterns. But those were the days when Geoffrey Rush was the waiter who brought me food and Anthony LaPaglia was the man who sold me shoes: no surprise then that the future Treasurer of the State was on hand to drive a chap about. Village life.

Then came the big risk. I moved to the country to be near my ancient parents till they accepted the move to the Twilight Farm.

> Life took some planning. To make use of the nearly empty cars that go everywhere all the time takes a certain local political skill.
>
> At first I lived near a general store, so day-to-day supplies were a short walk away. Now the parents have gone to join the saints in glory and I live instead on the main road that links the McLaren Vale vignoble to the Adelaide Hills and the rest of the South Mount Lofty Ranges. No shop; no bus, and cabs are unaffordable if indeed they could ever find me . . .

Same happened, though much later, with his lust for motorbikes. On a Hills road. Yamaha 850. Doing 300 kilometres an hour. The scene is pure, reckless devil-dabbling Philip. At this lick, his bones are shifting under his skin. He may not be faster than time, but he's seen more of its magic motion than most. Something (Philip isn't certain what) made him glance down at the speedometer. 'That was it,' Philip said. 'I swore never to ride a bike again.' He was no teenager at the time – actually about fifty-six. And, furthermore, trust Philip to mention he'd borrowed the bike from a known murderer, a 'nasty, evil man'.

Philip's willingness to adapt is stronger than most. He can take the meaning of the word 'jamming' from music and apply it to other aspects of his life. This takes more than the average time spent listening. Watching. Observing. 'I learnt pretty quickly people all have patterns in their lives,' he says.

> They drive around in empty cars and they actually like having somebody with them. So if you go to someone respectfully, and learn what people do, and say: 'Are you going to the shops again this week?' – 'Yeah, yeah, do you want a ride?' And it suits. I learnt to shop more carefully, once a fortnight. I've got no car, no TV and I've never had a credit card.

Philip sits in the perfumed garden of the Yangarra vineyards. He does live in a wonder of the world, make no mistake. The beauty is fresh and shimmering, painted only with natural colours. Little else speaks of riches gathered in sixty-eight years, which only amplifies his words. 'I'm not very interested in property. Apart from books and instruments. The 1927 Gibson. Other guitars. Amplifiers. I have no property other than papers and ideas.'

Local MP, Leon 'Biggles' Bignell, puts it best of all: 'He's had an outstanding life. That's what he's got to show for it all.'

CHAPTER 29

Winemakers Judge Philip

'I will leave you with the thought that White is a wine writer and worldwide there might be half a dozen more.'
– David Farmer, of Glug wines

Placing Philip in the pantheon of wine writers is not as easy as it might seem. Plenty of influential and astute industry insiders and outsiders nominate him as the best in Australia and somewhere in an imaginary international Top 20. But his facility for making enemies and sharpening the short sword of truth, as he sees it, places him in muddy waters. 'He's pissed off a lot of people' could be a line in the chorus of a song in a *South Park* musical about his life. While winemakers like Brian Croser are big enough to shrug off a Philip barrage or three, and heap praise upon his work, others are not so forgiving.

So, one has to hunt around for a way to accurately measure his weight. David Farmer, who runs the online winemaker-merchant Glug based in the Barossa and has been in the business for more than forty years, says: 'I remain perplexed that many, and I mention The Wine Communicators as an example, do not seem to have recognised the importance of Philip's art, or if they did, excluded him.' It is Farmer's next sentence that gives the true lie of the land: 'There may be history, though, of which I am unaware.' That touches an industry nerve that is directly connected to Philip's way with his Viking sax – a short sword, best for a fearless warrior for hand-to-hand combat in any given battle. Farmer is as good an example as any of those who can see beyond the smoke and flying gristle of feuds between producers and critics. Here he is in a Glug online article, published 27 June 2005.

> Perhaps our best wine writer is Philip White of the Adelaide *Advertiser*, which means few eastern states readers get to read his column and discover the intensity that shines through in his writing.
>
> We caught up for lunch the other day and were pleased to find age has not diminished his passionate attitude to take on causes and promote change in the wine industry.
>
> In 1981 he became the founding editor of the Adelaide-based *Winestate*, an excellent consumer magazine which is, of course, still going strong. The early editions are collector's items as the tasting panel includes such luminaries as John Stanford, Max Schubert and Wolf Blass.
>
> Then he went to edit the *Wine & Spirit Buying Guide*, which was in Sydney and had been started by Len Evans and initially was edited by John Parkinson, another industry legend who is now at the direct marketer, Cellarmasters.
>
> In those days we all assumed the *Winestate* would fold and the *Wine & Spirit Guide*, which outsold *Winestate* four to one, would prevail. Evans at this time was a consultant to the magazine on $4000 per month. It takes a bold man to sack Evans but that is what White did; a career move that would have finished lesser people. Then it was to the *National Times* as wine writer where they moved aside James Halliday to make room. The paper closed in 1988 but by then Piers Ackerman attracted him to the *Advertiser* where he has remained. Asked about the most significant causes he has pushed, White nominated the following: championing the use of screw caps as the best closure

going back to the days at *Winestate*; the dislike of American oak with its unnatural coconut aroma and wishes for it to be banned; objecting strongly to the use of added acids to wine because it gives an unnatural taste; and foresaw early (long before the rest of us) that Australian wines had enormous export appeal. He dates this view on exports to 1982–1983, helped by talks with Paul Jaboulet, of the famous French company, who was staggered by the quality of Australian shiraz, which made him believe that this variety would lead the way.

There were few believers back then and while exports were slowly lifting White was convinced by 1988 that they would finally take off. Listening to his long career we tend to the view that his great achievement was slowing the destructive vine-pull scheme of the mid 1980s and making enough people realise it was mad. As one grower said to White at the time: 'I pulled out my grandfather's garden today.'

We asked for a piece of advice for consumers and then the wine industry and were offered: 'Travel a fair bit and buy wine true to the dirt as the rest is Coca-Cola, and, quality is going down and the punter is not a mug and will eventually walk away if they are ripped off.'

David Farmer kindly gave permission for the edited replay of his article, and recommended a look at the start of one of the greatest tasting notes ever written, the opening lines of a long-tasting note on the Grange 2008 by Philip White:

This smells like an old slate gravestone covered with lichen. In the summer. Beneath, you can also smell the old dead Lutheran way down there.

They smell a bit like ancient linen in a cupboard not opened for generations. A good place to learn what I mean is the cemetery at Salem, by the Bremer east of Callington.

Farmer hit a big nail on the head with another Glug piece on the importance of writing talent over technical savvy:

> There are not many wine writers but there are hundreds of wine journalists and bloggers and I wonder how they do not die of boredom writing article after article about what they found when they visited winery ABC and always ending with half-a-dozen tasting notes. For decades I subscribed to *American Gourmet* partly for the wine writing of Gerald Asher who never bothered with tasting notes though you wanted to go to Tuscany after reading his article on Chianti, the people and the food.
>
> I was thinking along these lines while reading an article in the UK *Telegraph* by Michael Deacon: 'Roger Ebert: a critic of rare brilliance' (5 April 2013): 'A good critic is more than someone who happens to have an opinion. He's more than someone who happens to have an expert knowledge of his field. He's a performer. Because a good piece of criticism isn't a buyers' guide. It isn't facts and specifications and pros and cons, on the one hand, on the other hand, three out of five. It isn't best ever, worst ever, all-time top 10 . . . The critic's opinion isn't necessarily better than anyone else's. But his writing should be.'

'I will leave you with the thought,' says David Farmer, 'that White is a wine writer and worldwide there might be half a dozen more.'

RICK BURGE

> 'Never dull, sometimes wrong. Often intriguing. Always exhilarating.'

The year is 1982. Philip is based in Sydney, editing the *Wine & Spirit Buying Guide*. Winemaker Rick Burge is a self-described Young Turk, then running a vineyard for Brown Brothers in

Rutherglen, Victoria. He was a wine judge at an event at Sydney's newly minted Rocks, alongside the much-admired industry pioneer David Hohnen from Cape Mentelle in Margaret River. 'I'll never forget that day,' Burge says.

> It struck me they were their own people. Because Philip said he wanted my opinion of the wines, not what I thought might be the thing to say. So I learned not to be coerced, not to have this pack mentality. If David didn't like a wine or thought it was simple, he'd say: 'Guys, if you like the wine go ahead and give it that score, but I'm going lower.'

Burge, who sold Burge Family Winemakers in 2018 and retired to continue his ongoing battle with cancer, is a big fan.

> Philip's writing was such that I'd re-read it because it was written so well. It's as if it was 3D writing. He painted pictures; you put yourself in that situation. The other thing that struck me was his almost oxy-acetylene intellect. What I noticed about him was he always introduced a human element. You almost felt you knew more about the winemaker and his wife and his thoughts on politics or whatever than the wine itself. But that's what made the wine interesting because you felt how much he knew about what the guy had put into the wine. He would name wineries that he thought were awful, referring to one where 'you're always guaranteed a glass of industrial swill'.
>
> Philip didn't suffer fools – nothing wrong with that. He was erudite on so many bloody subjects. His intellect was absorbing all this material. Never dull. Sometimes wrong. Often intriguing. Always exhilarating. He was a name-dropper but he had every right to do it. It wasn't as if he'd met them just the once at a function, he knew them well. Philip was quite quiet about those connections. He never bragged about them. Those sorts of people were interested in Philip, because he was so well-connected and

> erudite. His comments on politicians are so astute and up to the mark. Philip would be quite famous if it was San Francisco, Berlin, London perhaps. Paris. I can imagine him having a drink with Keith Richards, hanging out on some Rue Whatever. But he chose to stay in Adelaide.
>
> His writing when he was stone-cold sober was his dullest. When he was pretty well cut he was at his most sarcastic and sometimes ugly. When he was just half cut I could read for hours, he was just so entertaining.

Rick remembers Philip could be a striking dresser; that when he made an entrance on certain random occasions, all heads would turn his way. One night, winemaker Peter Barry walked in dressed as the Pope, in very convincing robes, followed by Philip, who was in Cardinal Pell-type clothing. 'They tore up the Universal Bar on Rundle Street that night.'

> I think I knew more about Philip than he knew about me, but he always gave me oxygen and respect for who I was and didn't try to categorise me, didn't pigeonhole me. He loved our semillon, in particular. He was Hemingway-like in his ability to drink quite heavily and still function, and as an intellectual. Erudite, making sense. The true alcoholic will drink wine below their station. Philip wouldn't do that. If the drink was no good, he'd say I'm not drinking this shit, and go off and make a coffee.

Rick Burge remembers the early days, 'back when the top winemakers all drove Range Rovers and wore moleskins'. He is happy to see the change to Audis and designer clothes, but worries a little about what will happen when the current generation of wine writers goes. One light he sees is the abundance of bloggers, who seem to be diluting the 'quiet control' the prestigious winemakers exert over wine critics these days.

Their drawback is that their palates can't go back to the 80s or the 90s or even a 2008 wine, because they weren't born then. However they are connecting with what young people are drinking.

WILMA MCLEAN

Philip has a good relationship with many winemakers. But the larger-than-life Bob McLean, who died of liver cancer in 2015, had a special place in Philip's heart. Philip describes an early meeting: 'McLean was a jolly soul. The big fella with the neat beard – a rarity then – and the gravelly voice; a backslapper and hander-out of cigars.' Wilma McLean, Bob's widow, notes that Philip and Bob were similar characters.

> They were both pretty ebullient. Colourful, loved to tell stories. They bounced off each other. I remember one night the boys were all sitting round having a few drinks. They had no musical instruments so they made things up and started a band. They were all in very good voice. Bob decided he was a drummer.
>
> Philip often stayed over and he would get up in the morning, in his blue dressing gown, and invariably have a riesling at about 9 o'clock. Lots of stories, lots of laughter. And Philip has such a wonderful laugh, it is contagious. He has the most incredible head, fabulous memory, very articulate. He is a caring person although he tries to put up this very hard shell. His poetry is amazing; he's a very rounded person. His drinkster.com has been absolutely wonderful. A very special friend to both of us.

Bob McLean made a huge impact wherever he went, putting St Hallett Wines on the map and acting as international ambassador for Australian wine.

Later, he and Wilma established their Barr Eden Vineyard on

Mengler Hill, producing riesling, mataro, grenache and shiraz. Wilma:

> We met Philip in the early 70s; we had many crazy times. I'm thinking of Bob's fortieth birthday – which he wasn't going to have. Philip came and observed that the place looked really familiar to him. And we found out why. It was close to where he'd lost his car some time before, a light-blue Valiant ex-police car. He loved that car dearly, but forgot where he left it. It had been parked at his uncle's place. I remember he was so happy because he finally got his car back again.

Philip's version:

> My 1977 Valiant. It was the night Bob and I went on a pub crawl. We ended up in Macclesfield. I don't know where I woke up next morning, but my car wasn't with me. I was looking for that car for weeks. I eventually found it near the McLeans' property at an uncle's place. It was my work car. It was a powder-blue police pursuit Valiant sold in the days when they covered up the holes from the missing flashing lights apparatus with a new vinyl roof.
>
> It had been hot-rodded in town at the back of the jail there. A very fast car, 150 mile an hour, man, oh yeah. Had all the cops' pursuit gadgets, like heavy-duty suspension and all that shit. That was a really good car.

STEPHEN PANNELL

Stephen Pannell is one of Philip White's favourites, and vice-versa, not least because both are champions of the grenache revival.

> If you ask most winemakers who is the best wine writer in Australia the answer is Philip White. He has a great love for wine and the people who grow, make and drink it. His introduction to the Grange book he created with Milton is my favourite piece

of wine writing. It's evocative and beautiful. He has often been controversial and we all need and value his contributions to the Australian wine landscape.

Pannell also brings out the swaggering best in Philip, who once rhapsodised that the winemaker was:

> A bit like, say, virtuoso guitarist Andrés Segovia, but a Segovia who, having played brilliant concert-hall classical and flamenco guitar for one lifetime, suddenly sheds a million ornate, hard-learned and rehearsed trills and arpeggios and counterpoints to switch to good old 12-bar blues and starts again. With about 95 per cent fewer tricks and flourishes. Fewer dots. Back to three chords. This is what confounds those pretenders and winey blatherskites.

DAVID O'LEARY

David O'Leary from O'Leary Walker Wines in the Clare Valley:

> My first impressions haven't changed, he had a cheeky demeanour and he's still got that. He loved wines and wanted to learn more, as we all did. We all learned together. I was keen on regional wine shows, and Philip was my go-to journalist judge.
>
> People then weren't giving these local shows attention and now they're incredibly strong. We saw what happened at McLaren Vale and Philip was pretty much at the coalface of regionality. His passion for soils and microclimates has never changed and it's correct, been proven over the years – eighty per cent of the great wines are made from the site and the soil.
>
> He'd come and judge at Clare, he was funny. He'd tease out the great wines and has always been a deep thinker. Philip's one of the greatest journalists ever. Entertaining. Thoughtful. Brilliant. He was never frightened to upset a few people. It's not about who

> was right and who was wrong, it's about how great the Australian wines were and look where we've come. He's been a big part of that journey. With the records and tapes he's got of Max Schubert [Penfolds legend] and other people he could write fifteen books. He really can sort out the wheat from the chaff.

Philip was notorious for forming genuine friendships with the very people who were his prey. Regardless of your tightrope skills, it is always fraught. One scathing review of an important wine and, suddenly, you have a foe who could lose money or reputation.

It could be called 'blind and deaf honesty'. The reality is Philip wanted to get to know everyone in the realm – especially the giants.

CHAPTER 30

Deadlines Philip Knew

'Philip runs his own show and works to his own deadlines.'
– Colin James, journalist

Photographer Milton Wordley:

> I found out about the less predictable side of Philip when I asked him to write the words for my coffee table book of photographs, *A Year in the Life of Grange*, which retailed for $785, the same price as a bottle of 2008 Penfolds Grange. It was always going to be expensive, as I wanted the book – like Grange – to be a 100% South Australian product, printed here and not in China. Initially, he didn't want to do it because he had a possible commission from another publisher in Melbourne. Then one day he rang and said he'd rather work with me 'because you'll let me be me'. He'd also made a promise to Max Schubert that one day he'd write the story of Penfolds wine, and, therefore, of Grange. Finally, he felt ready to fulfil that promise.
>
> Philip's very fussy about what he writes and has a little trouble with deadlines. He was a little bit late for my book, well a lot late actually. For a month, I was very worried that Philip wasn't producing anything and I had quite a tight deadline. I was getting the odd email from Philip that he was not happy being pushed. The tone was 'when you get it, you'll get it' but he wasn't rude. But once Philip got the opening essay/poem right, it flowed. It is the most amazing piece of writing, as many wine writers have mentioned to me.

Milton adds: 'Wine writer Tim White (no relation) always reminds me to tell Philip it is the best passage on Australian wine he's ever read.'

> *Grange arose. It came from the*
> *South Australian dust through the*
> *spirit of a Barossa Valley stable*
> *boy, the son of a blacksmith.*
>
> *Grange took its power from a wine*
> *empire founded at the far end*
> *of the Earth by an English doctor*
> *and his mighty winemaking wife;*
> *its architecture from a team of*
> *the most radical wine scientists*
> *ever assembled.*
>
> *Grange took its oak from the*
> *forests of Missouri; its fruit from a*
> *vine which evolved on the slopes*
> *of the Rhône.*
>
> *An enduring emblem of creative*
> *Australian confidence, Grange was*
> *forged in the ashes of the most*
> *destructive war our lonesome blue*
> *planet had known.*
>
> Philip White, *A Year in the Life of Grange*, p. 4

Nick Ryan is now all grown up, and a distinguished wine writer himself, but he revered the legendary wine writer when he was a boy.

> I knew the byline before I knew the man. It was actually my late partner Sarah, a cadet at the *Advertiser*, who met him first. I used to love the stories she told; like the story about one of her first jobs. The editor would say: 'Here's a cab charge to the Exeter and one back. Philip White's late on his copy. Go down there with a pen and pad, get his copy and bring it back.' These were the great old days. It wasn't hard to find Philip.
>
> Sarah just had to sit there in the corner of the front bar of the Exeter, hand over the pad and the pen and wait until she could take the finished article back to the office for the deadline.

David Sly started editing Philip White's copy in the nineties.

> He would argue to the death and say he's never missed a deadline, but from where I sat, he would more or less invent his own deadline. The funniest of all time came when I was absolutely under the pump – this is pre-mobile phones or early mobile days, so stories were largely still being faxed through to me. Best Philip excuse of all time – he was with a bunch of winemaker mates on a houseboat on the Murray and it was marooned on a sandbar and he had to find a rowing boat to get to the shore and then wave down a passing farmer to take him to the nearest town with a post office so he could fax his copy to me. I thought: Why bother even printing the wine yarn, just that houseboat story was good enough on its own to publish. The pirate poet that is Philip came to the fore that day. Again, any wait was worth it.
>
> There was a beautiful music to Philip's best work. He'd be able to thread a lot of dense background into the story of why does this glass of wine fascinate me and it was seamless the way he'd

> pull it all together and you could see the depth of his curiosity in those great columns.

Colin James, of the *Advertiser*, adores Philip. But he does not hold back in his assessment of his less-disciplined side.

> Tony Love and I got given the job of managing him and Philip is not someone who can be managed. Philip runs his own show and works to his own deadlines. Eventually he became too hard to handle.

He adds: 'If you're going to do wine writing you've got to not have prejudices against certain people.'

Now a freelancer, Sly tackles the issue of Philip having 'no journalistic filter' – born of a professional requirement to cross-check sources of contentious and possibly costly libel claims.

> There was a coterie of mates at the Exeter, and they were getting in Philip's ear. He was ruffling a lot of feathers, being very outspoken about things, and it became clear that there were Philip's mates and there were people outside. You were in or you were out. Sometimes he had good, strong reasons for disliking what people were doing with their wine. But it became apparent that if you crossed one of Philip's mates, it was going to come full circle. I would receive copy and think, this cannot be published. That's a hand grenade with the pin taken out. You can't put that in.
>
> Philip was also doing a second column, Pure White, for the Saturday edition, because Philip was prepared to be completely outspoken and be bold. That would come straight from the front bar of the Exeter. It was always interesting, never a dull moment. This was pure scuttlebutt. I would keep going back to him: 'Philip, we can't publish this. Where's the evidence of this?' And he would say: 'It's the truth, because this guy told me.' I'd reply: 'Philip, that is not a defence for libel.'

Philip would push back. It was as if I was challenging his integrity. 'You don't trust me, I trust this guy who told me and I take issue with that.' 'Philip, you've got something called the law. It's not about the vibe if you say that and can't produce evidence; that's an accusation that will take us to court.'

Again, it would always come in late, skating close to deadline. So you had to have an experienced sub-editor looking out for the unexploded hand grenades. There was an element of naiveté I suppose. It was reckless but there was no malice intended. It wasn't to 'get' people; he felt these things needed to be said. It might have been savage, but he believed it to be true. In all Philip's copy there was nothing disingenuous.

Mutual admiration: Philip with winemaker Stephen Pannell, and Rebecca Hocking, public relations.

Saving the Barossa and McLaren Vale: Philip with Kelly Vincent, politician, playwright and actor, who represented the Dignity Party in SA's Upper House from 2010 until 2018.

Philip, attending the Humbug Club at the Exeter Hotel, Rundle Street. It was started in 1859 by Jefferson Stow and George Isaacs, as a newsletter poking fun at hypocrisy and self-aggrandisement, and it grew into the Gawler *Bunyip* newspaper.

Philip and jeweller Albert Bensimon celebrating the legendary Saturday Table lunches (usually held weekly at T-Chow) at a party at the home of Paul and Vicki Nisenblat in the Adelaide Hills.

Philip with his beloved uncle Philip, an interior designer.

Media mates. Left to right: Dennis Atkins, Philip, Terry Plane.

Philip had a couple of flights in winemaker Tim Knappstein's Boeing Stearman, a plane used to train US Air Force pilots who were to fly Mustangs. Philip believes, 'You haven't lived until you've flown upside down over the Watervale Hotel at least once.'

Philip with second-eldest sibling Stephen, who has had a long and successful career in mining.

Mirage? Philip holding aloft a bottle of water . . .

Cartoonist George Grainger Aldridge (left) and Leon Bignell, Member for Mawson, which takes in McLaren Vale (right), on a visit to the Yangarra vineyard cottage following news of Philip's cancer diagnosis, 15 December 2018.

Undiluted love: A cancer-weary Philip melts into longtime friend Heath Cullen, who has worked with three-time Grammy winner Joe Henry, including on Cullen's latest album, *Springtime in the Heart*. 'Heath was just back from recording in California,' says Philip. 'He sat down here on the front porch at Yangarra and played the whole album for me.'

Blast: Under the weight of his Russian military fur hat, Philip makes light of one of his first blasts of chemo in January 2019. (Photo Leon Bignell)

Philip with his great friend, Steve Stacey.

Philip with winemaker Greg Trott, of Wirra Wirra, a key player in McLaren Vale's premium image and in the modern wine industry, early 2000s. 'Trotty was the first winemaker to get the importance of protecting the environment, and we revved each other up on that,' Philip says. 'He was one of the winemakers I was closest to.' Philip would like to be buried alongside Trotty in the Strout Road cemetery at Willunga.

CHAPTER 31

Bad Moon Rises

'I knew there was something seriously wrong.'
– Philip, on his health in early 2018

It was March 2018. As usual, days flying by too fast. Philip's mates were commenting on how unwell he looked. Some days he wasn't quite himself. As in his usual articulate, centred, assured self. On the bad days, he was even paler than usual, a bit unsteady. A tightening fistful of pains that had been niggling for years was heaving and rolling inside.

> I'd been putting off having a hernia in my left anterior groin area cut back in and everybody who saw it including the docs thought it was a piece of bowel, which is not uncommon, on the bend. I thought, This is getting tender and sore. Bad sleeps and nightmares and horrors and shit didn't help.

Word had passed around that the colt from No Regret was fading away. Philip might not see Christmas. Matter of fact, Philip did see Christmas. Plus many more months. But it was a close-run thing. And the Big Reprieve came at a funeral for a friend. Philip was paying respects to winemaker Drew Dowie, of Dowie Doole, who passed away peacefully, aged sixty-seven. He was standing next to a stranger who he thought resembled Charles Bronson in his portrayal of the avenging Apache in the film *Chato's Land*.

He had a black suit, white shirt and no tie; a black dirty comb-over. Not a big guy but charismatic. He commented on my Spanish leather cowboy boots. I asked him a question, and he told me he had been Drew Dowie's doctor. I replied: 'You're famous – you've been saving his life for the past twelve years. You must have a gap in your bookings.' He said: 'It's time to make it a long meeting.' Dr Mike Reid, of McLaren Vale Family Practice, has taken personal responsibility for my health since then.

Early December 2018. Philip was given a list of specialists and instructed to undergo seven scans 'really quickly . . . it's nearly Christmas, if we don't get you sorted, completely, you'll be gone in six weeks'. Philip laughs that rising falling laugh of his, a nervous tic.

When the doc had the scan results he told me to sit down and said: 'Houston, we have a problem. You are riddled with cancer.' I asked: 'What sort of cancer?' He replied: 'Some looks like it's come from your prostate.'

During that week of scans, we actually watched it get worse. It was rabid. Then he banged me straightaway with the female hormone, like a fake oestrogen, which switches off testosterone production. We'd discovered I had tumours everywhere. I started having the morning sickness immediately after that first infusion, which is a big thing, like another type of chemo. We've got it down from forty minutes to rapid but I will have to do that every week all my life.

The stuff that was in my pelvis, the doc said, was very old, many years old. Nobody was game to say how old. When they drained the juice, it stank. It was a miracle that my good thigh hadn't taken the sponge from my pelvis. I'd always been looking after this left leg. Been broken by a semi-trailer, broken the foot, car accidents. I've always favoured it.

What about his mates fearing he'd be dead last Christmas?

I didn't feel terminal to any degree, I knew there was something seriously wrong. Liver malfunction: I healed by cleansing myself with green vegetable juice. Most of my life the things I'd do to repair myself were not regarded with any respect. I was postponing getting a new GP after I moved from Mt Barker to Yangarra. After learning what they were scanning for, that kept me busy.

It wasn't until I got the prognosis that my brain changed gear. Like it suddenly reshuffled everything in thirty minutes. Like a different chip. Everything that had been important, the list of significant things got addressed, things that had worried me all my life, regular day-to-day things. All the things I'd been worried about were gone. I thought: I have to drop everything and fight this fucker somehow. I didn't know what that meant. I was quickly ill enough not to be able to write. It's like the battery I'd had for writing had been taken out. I had none of that energy. All the DNA had been thrown away. So I leant on Twitter, because it's one sentence. It also kept me a bit competitive. Because I've lost all my testosterone. So I'm very passive. Bizarre. No point worrying about it. Having had this good news, my brain rebalanced to where it was before the bad news. I want to write a book on grenache now my brain's better than my body. I can't walk at home because it's all dangerous. Can't exercise. I depend on my claw grabber stick for picking my socks up off the floor. I can't pull on a pair of pants because my fingernails all hurt, they've been killed by chemo. Lost three toenails. All black.

CHAPTER 32

Not Dead Yet

'I hope we are all in better shape than our mate Mr White.'
Milton Wordley in an email bulletin to friends

When it comes to terminal illness for a loved one, news flow is a blessing for friends and family. Surrounded by media mates, Philip took the opportunity to issue updates, usually emails through his photographer friend Milton Wordley.

One of the first emerged on 6 December 2018:

> Time for a more relaxed typeface.
>
> 1. Yesterday I completed my first week of intensive photon radiation therapy on the lumbar tumour. We now wait a week or so to begin measuring our success. This was very critical urgent treatment of a deadly alien. I am very pleased that the docs did so much to crash me through quick.
>
> 2. This cessation should ease my morning sickness and the need for related drugs and my mobility should gradually return.
>
> 3. The hormone therapy is working impressively on the metastasised floaters in my abdomen, also improving my mobility. I have also developed my mother's skin.
>
> 4. Big meeting with the incredible Pelvis Engineers and Sappers on Monday will carry on with serious quarrying plans following intensive 3-D mapping. If this pit is dug and my hip replaced the system may weaken enough that more radiation will be required.

(Mixed metaphor warning: not sure yet whether this is a quarrying operation or more of change of diff down the F1 pits.)

5. Depending on how all this goes, we hope to eventually get round to chemo.

Thank you all for your good wishes and assistance on so many levels. I am humbled and overwhelmed. Not dead yet.

12 DECEMBER 2018

Milton:

I hope we are all in better shape than our mate Mr White. He's asked me to forward you his latest news. We saw Philip with Annika the other night, he had just got some news re his current situation. Looks like they want to operate on his pelvis ASAP before they start on the chemo. He was a bit overwhelmed by the prospect of it, but in reasonably good spirit. Annika and Adrian are being fantastic support. For those who don't know Annika, she's an old friend of Philip's and the daughter of Settlement Wines founder, Vincenzo 'Enzo' Berlingieri. Together with Monica, me and my partner Anne-Marie, we are a sort of local support group doing hospital runs and other things.

Philip's bulletin:

Tentative: white exmess

1. Yesterday we had a meeting of part of my formidable War Room crew, four of us surrounded by vid screens, discussing the bones and tumours in a client in the form of me.

2. We are now committed to major surgery of my pelvis as soon as I can get a Flinders berth, which means any minute/day soon.

3. They will replace my good right femur with a new one during the rebuild of a collapsing cancerous socket in the hip. They

will quarry the cancer from the pelvis while they have it open, repack the cavity with antibiotic cement and then fit me a new reinforced diff: socket, ball joint, femur, etc.

This is a very long and risky operation.

A week ago, we had no idea this would become the first thing necessary. It is essential that it works. My pelvis is crumbling and soft, and the bone people can't believe that it hasn't collapsed to spill old cancerous stuff everywhere and break the artery.

4. If all goes smoothly, I can commence chemo in the middle of January. This is essential for all the other cancers. If something goes wrong, and that is postponed, I am in deeper shit.

5. Similarly, if there are complications which weaken my immune system after surgery, it may be too late to recommence beneficial radiation therapy on my deadly lumbar one tumour. I hate that fucker. I have finished the first course of that radiation, but it'll be a week or two before the success of that can begin to be measured. PS: The public health service I am getting at Flinders is mind-blowing in its scientific intensity and determination. Smooching sincere gratitude and love to all of you . . . you know who you are! My boundaries are a tad smudged and rattling right now, but I'm NOT DEAD YET!

Despite the rising fears, Philip maintained his droll sense of humour. Even as the scary scans kept throwing up bad news upon worse, he would send out missives like this on drinkster.com:

13 DECEMBER 2018

Sunset tonight over the Yangarra High Sands Grenache, across my back fence . . . after that dead-dry spring, it's been a wild and sinister few days of weather, restive and unpredictable . . . laundry all over the lawn . . . the dam is still way down and there's been bad frost in some of the lower blocks . . . These young hares, meanwhile, have finally ceased boxing the living shit out of each other. The jack spent the morning whacking a male adversary then this jill he thought he'd won – she's bigger – bashed the hell out of him for dessert before commencing the formal peace ritual. Read bonking: working on raising a leveret or two.

LATE DECEMBER 2018

After two over-confident days fresh out of surgery I had 48 hours of deep sleep and lots of very effective drugs. Adrian presented me yesterday with his dad's Zimmer frame, which is helping me move and assisting my leg rebuild. I'm not over-confident, but I reckon I can soon live without it. I'm hoping to move home soon. The goat curry Annika's working on for tonight is a terrible tease.

I went for a twenty-metre walk this arvo. I'll let you know my next step when I know. War Room meeting mid-week. I've recommenced hormone therapy (just in time); more spine zapping as soon we can; then chemo. Thank you all for your care and support: forgive me for hiding a while in this tricky time, I have been pretty crook but all things considered I am one very lucky unit.

Flinders Hospital is incredible. All the best for the New Year.

31 JANUARY 2019

They got me through all that pelvis action and out of Flinders before Christmas Day.

Now we know what my new diff/axle assembly looks like (F1 x motocross) – meat, and having learned a fair bit about how well it handles they've also hastened the radiation of the unit and I'm already halfway through a week of intensive nuking, to kill any lurkers remaining after that astonishing rebuild. In other words, the bone/chassis people have for now handed to the nuclear people control of the arsenal/ballet/logistics thing aimed at opposing parties within the State.

The nukers meanwhile remain obsessed with their forensic biffo of the lumbar #1 tumour, which will follow the clearing of the hips much sooner than had been thought possible. The hormone adjustment folks meanwhile stand muttering in the aircraft carrier's laundry, concerned about the PMT and morning sickness symptoms which their removal of my testosterone incurs, and about how the pelvic nukers are now exaggerating that, like vom. Like total VOM! Like nuke can make you feel sick. It turns the vom knob way up, even if it started at 10.

When all these incidents are exhausted, we can commence chemo. Praised be his precious and healing name. The Berlingieri Glass Shin Wordley Aldinga Fringe continues with amazing precision and generosity to pump stalwart assistance up my hill. Between getting me in and out of Flinders almost daily, replacing intensive care and accommodation and eventually getting me resettled at home, these people are fair dink angels of mercy. They can suddenly accept a change of gears, like this week when all my hospital plans were suddenly replaced with something completely different and twice as fast.

5 FEBRUARY 2019

A new routine begins. The week of radiation of the rebuilt pelvis made me quite ill; a new installation of Degarelix in the belly fat intensified the morning sickness; for the first time I felt lost, pissed off. I nearly forgot my luck. Top goodness: the brilliant chemo and radiation divisions have agreed on a way of overlaying their ordnance so we can begin chemo before the March deadline but recommence nuking that sinister bastard of a tumour protruding from lumbar #1.

The nukers are very wary of frying the tattered old spinal cord, so they're cutting the radiation by half and doubling the number of zaps, with a day off between each one.

It's good to be having a few days rest now before it all starts again. My appetite returns. The new diff is running in very well, all things considered. I find myself in the kitchen, forgetfully without Zimmer or stick. And for the first time I was just now able to lean over far enough to dry the toes on my right foot, which is a luxury. Road transport hurts: I save most of my daily quota for Flinders trips, but hospital, not Ranges, dammit. The reward is time with my Beloved Transport Corps, which guarantees a refined level of conversation to counteract my medications and madness. A deep bow to you.

I am deeply grateful to everybody for all your encouragement and support. It humbles and overwhelms me while it gets on with firing my belly. Thank you, my dear friends. For a few decades there, I thought people who could read were dying out.

20 FEBRUARY 2019

Where have I been? What's the time?

Sometime in November I felt crook and with the deft diagnosis and advice from a brilliant local GP, ended up in the incredible cancer ward at Flinders. The excellent people there at the Cancer Research Centre (thank you, Lance Armstrong!) quite simply saved my life.

After a few days in intensive, recuperating from a huge pelvis quarrying and the fitment of half a new hip and leg, I went to stay with Berls [Annika Berlingieri] and Adrian Glass, who have a spare bedroom with an en suite fitted for handicapped people. I re-learned walking on Adrian's dad's spare Zimmer. On a crutch or stick now.

Freshly aware that I'm not alone, apart from being extremely sick, I am very well for an old bloke halfway through a long period of hormone-radio-chemo therapy and some pretty radical surgery . . . I feel like a building project manager, just keeping control of all the genius subbies, but still can't line up the right blocks for a proper column. My sensories have gone nuts . . . they rejected me. Evacuated. So far, most of my creative energy has gone into that building project, staying alive and posting the odd tweet. I have a grand troupe of helpers, friends and supporters from all over the ball, and have little idea of how to thank you for your care, feelings, time and generous gifts.

Top highlights of the last week were visits from beloved family, from sister and brothers and their families, to my last surviving uncle, Philip, and his brilliant daughters. Many of these people I'd not seen in many years. During which I'd been very wary of ever 'sleeping peacefully, surrounded by close family and friends'.

CHAPTER 33

Onward

'But here I am.'
Philip White

A year later, the widespread disbelief or astonishment, call it what you will, came whirling in. A fairly convincing facsimile of the Philip before cancer diagnosis was provoking comment. He looked so much healthier, though still clearly ailing. Colour back in his skin. Hair growing back. And dullness of the eyes had been replaced by shine. The daily and weekly grind of chemo and blood tests had given way to positive reports. Medical visits were spaced out – his blood appointments suspended for six months. Any walking aid had been left in a corner. While the old cocky gait may never make a comeback, Philip was back on his own two feet. However, he has been prone to the odd heavy fall or two. By August 2020, Philip was able to report to his fleet of volunteers:

> My mornings are still rocky, and probably always will be, I have enjoyed feeling more normal these last afternoons than I have since I first hit Flinders. That was a long way back down this torrid winding track. Apart from the regular hormone chemo, my medication consumption is nearly zero now; I don't have to eat tablets to feel hungry and eat food.
>
> Psychology still a tad ratty. Chemo remnants linger and nag. Brain's a bit like Swiss cheese some days.
>
> But here I am.

The health bulletins – always expressing gratitude – are a reminder that for all the seemingly miraculous progress, life can be rotten on a daily basis for the long-suffering patient. Mornings are almost invariably like a bad hangover, with vomiting and nausea. By 11 am, Philip is listening to music or radio and up for a conversation and a chat with the birds.

The positives and the gloomy reminders come in waves like this, Philip writes:

> The boss of my oncology, the fastidious Sina Vatandoust, has just sent me away for six months. He is visibly delighted at my improvement; that I survive, indeed. His assistant was sufficiently disbelieving of my recent blood that he rang the lab and had them reassure him, one reading after another. It went, 'That's encouraging . . . that's amazing! Are you sure?'
>
> 'You will live with the reality of cancer for the rest of your life,' he then advised. 'After what you've endured, having got this far, you will learn to adapt.'

Every day can be a shock or just a stutter of bother and inconveniences. For example, still waiting for the delivery of an emergency neck/wrist buzzer: 'I'll feel much more secure with that.' Cancer complications to his immune system mean Philip has to be careful about human contact, beyond the demands of dealing with COVID-19. He would love to be able to call a taxi, but feels he cannot take the risk of getting an unclean vehicle. He asks of Milton Wordley: 'Who's that cabbie you found who used to get me to and fro the Exeter? I might trust him.'

Another day, another mini-shock:

> The doc's also worried about my heart again, so in a week or two I'll need to get to the Daw Park Repat for another scan . . . something about a build-up of calcium in the tubes: we'll face that when it comes.

'No need for panic, Whitey,' he advised, 'but it'd be terrible if after all this hard work and treatments we lose you because we forgot your pump.' Doc never forgets. Blood pressure and heart rate's ideal. No sign of the tumours that were in the lungs, the lymph, the liver, and were creeping up my spine toward my brain. Pelvis reconstruction work is all tickety-boo.

The seesaw creaks on. Philip takes it all on with calm stoicism that few expected in the beginning. Milton Wordley has witnessed the dragon-fire that could spring from Philip in the pre-cancer era. 'I do think the cancer has changed him,' Milton says.

He doesn't let rip with the same level of oaths and curses when he has something to say about somebody he didn't like. For example, James Halliday. In the past, when you mentioned Halliday, you'd get a rant. Now, nothing. He's a lot more vulnerable now. There are two to three different personalities within Mr White. If you read his writing, sometimes you think: Philip didn't write that.

18 MARCH 2020

Philip writes:

I had a big challenge Thursday. The palliative care people came.

A lovely man interviewed me at length about minute details of my incanceration (sic) which I'd never considered. It was very confronting, frank and, finally, relieving.

He promises assistance I'd never imagined, and already gave me good advice about eating (sick of baby food) and basic housekeeping and other stuff I can't really attend to. I can't bend over to get stuff from the floor, for example. Or make the friggin bed. He helped Ninja Doc rewrite my terrifying canker of painkiller and steroid business, a rococo pharma regime which had built up over six months of well-intentioned experts adding to the list.

The new Jenny Craig model leaves me feeling better within 48 hours of the changeover.

We had clean exchanges about dealing with other people's grief at my condition, then my likelihoods bad and good, and began discussing a civilised death, so I have less to worry about. It won't be next week, but it's doubtful it'll be 2050, if you're one who likes deadlines.

Prospective longevity varies by the minute in this business. Buy some short-term comfort, lose some long. Go for more long term, and make the short hurt more. That's okay: it's worked for five months longer than was first suggested.

I'm not giving up.

Anyway, this was a big change of head after many monotonous months, and I'm very pleased and comforted.

Such things are worth an extra letter!

Besides, I gotta practise. I want to write a fast book before I face some sort of column again, if I remain uncarked.

Blessings, and thanks for the reassuring tide of vibe.

Whitey

In his own write:
Selected columns, 1984–2018

Adelaide Recast as the Monaco of the South

NATIONAL TIMES, 28 DECEMBER 1984 – 3 JANUARY 1985

It's a strange, exciting thing to watch world formula-one driving champion Niki Lauda squint down Adelaide's genteel Dequetteville Terrace, wondering just how much faster than 300 km/h he'll be able to go there, and how many gears he'll have to change to get around the corner into Wakefield Road.

Somehow the droll order that dominates this little city's traffic *demands* to see Lauda blast down the street, the shriek of his 800 horsepower 1.5 litre formula one scattering the Commodores like a peregrine falcon loose in a cage of canaries.

Adelaide, you see, needs a kick in the pants. The heady Dunstan days of wine and roses have faded completely. The roses have faded, anyway. Where then we found the *New Yorker* magazine calling the place possibly the best planned, best governed and most contented metropolis anywhere in the world, we now see more of local columnist Des Colquhoun aptly writing: 'Adelaide – the city that grew up to become a town.' The place has contentedly slid back into the mud. Rather than a premier prone to recite poetry from astride an elephant's trunk in the local zoo, the croweaters have an unassuming bloke who's probably jogging past the front door right now, unnoticed, training for his next marathon. Meanwhile, in the city of leafy courtyards, the chardonnay flows on.

But Premier John Bannon has just handed it its most dramatic change of personality since Donnie walked into Parliament in pink hotpants: in late October or November 1985, there will be a formula one grand prix through the tidy burgh's tree-lined streets. There'll be one each year for the next seven years.

Bannon zipped off to London to finalise the deal with Bernie Ecclestone, the chief executive of the Formula One Constructors Association. Adelaide is still trying to understand just what all this will mean.

[Philip then introduced Bill O'Gorman, manager of Sandford Travel in North Adelaide, and a former racing driver 'whose career involved more brick walls and hay bales than chequered flags'. Philip's article continues.]

During a few convivial drinks with alderman Wendy Chapman, O'Gorman came over a bit sarcastic, suggesting the South Australian 150th celebrations in 1986 would amount to a little more than 'a few knitting competitions and a period costume ball'.

In response to Chapman's challenge that he come up with a better idea, O'Gorman decided there'd be no better method of putting Adelaide on the international map than staging a formula one grand prix – in the streets.

'Wendy's a very persuasive person,' he explains, 'which is why she's now Lord Mayor.'

[The killer lines:]

O'Gorman: 'See, the Victorians wanted a formula one race at Sandown, and they even got the money out of their government to build the circuit. But, as Bernie Ecclestone said: 'Why would I come all that way to have this on a racetrack? It'd be easier for me to put some gum trees on Brand's Hatch, call it the Australian Grand Prix, and nobody'd know where it was. After all, they had the Swiss Grand Prix in France for 10 years.

'You've got to understand that people want to see a city.'

Edited version, by permission, Philip Christopher White.

Striking a Fine Balance

ADVERTISER, 29 JULY 1992

I wake up in the morning, see. I do my exercises and find a nice clean shirt and give it a bit of an iron and I flatten a tie while I'm at it. I have a wash in the shower and do my teeth and wonder why I don't get a haircut. Shake a few calls out of the answering machine. Hate it. Get dressed and bung on an old Stones record. Catch a taxi off to the tasting at the Hyatt. Socks feel a bit crunchy, but they look okay. I cleaned my boots. I'm feeling pretty good as I walk through the door into the Adelaide Hills and Eden Valley Winemakers tasting exhibition, but I'm starving. 'Light buffet lunch', they said on the invite.

About 12.30, I start on the wines. First thing is some winemaker comes up and says: 'Jeez, Philip, you gotta tie on.' Next thing another says: 'Gotta tellya, Phil, I couldna recognised ya.' These are blokes who get their wives to do their ironing. I ignore 'em.

I've always been a bit tough on the winemakers of the southern Mt Lofty Ranges because I reckon they've got no idea about names. The whole world wants them to use a name that's on the map. The map says the hills that go from Victor to Truro are the southern Mt Lofty Ranges. Now they've decided to call themselves the Adelaide Hills and Eden Valley Winemakers. At least, the Eden Valley's on the map. But Heggie's and Hill Smith Estate aren't in the Eden Valley. They're in the Barossa Ranges. Different Valley really.

I've always been a bit tough on 'em, so this time, I go: 'Okay, Philip, just do the business. Get the wines done and you can have a nice lunch.' Next thing, another one comes up and says: 'Good

Lord, is that Philip White?' It didn't go upwards at the end like a question. So I know straight away it isn't a question. Carry on with the business. Sniff, scribble. Slurp, scribble. Spit, scribble. Except for the really good ones, you let the really good ones run straight on down.

[*Philip continues to question the 'regionality' relevance of the show, before batting away comments about his appearance.*]

Then up comes one of the famous names: 'Well, well,' he says, wearing the shirt his wife's slaved over, 'I have to say I woulda not recognised ya someone hadna pointed you out,' he says. 'You look different every time we see you.' 'Yep,' I say, real polite. 'And you always look exactly the same.'

The thing about the Mt Lofty Ranges is the remarkable fact that they produce, year in, year out, the best chardonnay and pinot noir grapes in South Australia.

Look at the chardonnays. Other than the Mountadam, which I always reckon is the best in Australia, they've all got great grapes, but the wood's just a bit wrong. Like in most other areas, they give 'em just a bit too much, or it's a bit too resiny. But they're lovely, apart from a few brumbies, one of the best sets in the country. From the Norman's Chais Clarendon 91 (clean, crisp, wood) through the Birdwood Estate 90 (new 'un, rich, creamy, oaky), the stunning Petaluma 90 from Piccadilly (smoky, delicious, complex) to the Shaw & Smith 91 from Kuitpo (smoky, tart, good potential) they're a bunch of beauties. 'Yes, mate, I've put on a tie especially for the day. I was hoping not to attract too much attention.'

Then there was Lenswood. 'No, dear, I haven't lost weight. But you've got plenty of condition on.' Lenswood is easily our most exciting new wine region. If you can call a 10-year-old wine region new.

The wines are utterly stunning and improving year by year. The Lenswood Chardonnays of Stafford Ridge 90 (greenpeach and lime, very woody) and Henschke 90 (great cool area fruit, smoky oak) are magnificent, despite their prominent oak, yet just a hint of what this region will produce with further maturation in the vineyards.

'Yes, mate, I have quite a few ties, actually. Look, I reckon I'd've got less attention here if I'd come with my fly down.'

'Here, mate, take this tie. It's a Givenchy.'

Lenswood.

Edited version, by permission, Philip Christopher White.

Bottling Grapes of Wrath

ADVERTISER, 5 AUGUST 1992

Pretentious winos like me get bristly around the collar when wine companies send out press releases quoting other wine critics. You've been buying and praising some grumpy little blighter's booze for a decade without a word of thanks and suddenly he sends you a press release. He has paid some flash Harry a grand to write the damned thing and the best it does is quote Hugh Johnson or Robert Parker or some other callow hack from parts foreign, telling you the wine is good, usually in language you wouldn't let dribble from your quill in a blue funk. Rubbish bin.

Last month, Brian Croser broke all those rules by sending me a press release which quotes me. This caused a fit of the ego, a sudden rush of water to the head. I tended to overlook it at first. The quote looked accurate, there was a bottle attached, and the rest of the tome read as if Croser had written it himself.

I should explain to those who came in late that Brian Croser is the proprietor of Petaluma (one of the best and most expensive of our boutique wineries), is probably the industry's most outspoken and controversial spokesman and educator, is chairman of judges at the Adelaide Wine Show, has an ego that makes mine look dehydrated and writes about wine (not always his own) in the Melbourne *Age*. That paper's regular wine critic, the author Mark Shield, says: 'I don't make wine to compete with him – he shouldn't be competing with professional journos like me.'

Modesty saw me overlook Croser's press release. I thought I'd stick the wine in the next masked tasting and let the quality do the talking. But on Saturday at the Coonawarra winemakers' extremely popular exhibition at the Norwood Hotel (congratulations all) numerous key winefolk from that region complained about James Halliday's wine column in the *Weekend Australian*. I went home and read it. Then I read it again. Then I dragged out Croser's press release and read it more thoroughly. Not only did James omit my quote (of course) but his yarn seemed to very closely follow Brian's.

James Halliday is as controversial a wine character as Croser. He is a fellow wine judge, makes his own expensive wine in Victoria and comments weekly in the *Australian*.

A Week of Weird Happenings

ADVERTISER, 23 SEPTEMBER 1992

People expect astonishing things of a wine columnist. Like a name for a cow. I'm at this utterly beautiful little wine estate, Greenock Creek, while Michael and Annabelle Waugh, the proprietors, are off on Kangaroo Island, celebrating his 50th birthday. I've already heard that he ate two dozen oysters and a seafood platter for breakfast, with just a shot of smoked trout for dessert and I thought 'damned good breakfast for a 50-year-old' as I looked their new Brahman heifer in the eye and wondered what in the world we would call her. Annabelle says it should be Indian and I immediately suggest Shiva, the Destroyer and the Reproducer. I had a Valiant called Shiva, named after the great writer, Shiva Naipaul. Shiva, rest his soul (or recycle it) was a damned fine car in anybody's language. Off it went, in the end, to the organ donors and any cow that goes half as fast as it would be a champion. So Shiva still seems the best name. I'll bet the poor brute ends up with something like Daphne or Cynthia and several children from fathers she'll never meet. At least she'll do it all gazing out over one of the cutest little shiraz vineyards on earth.

[*Philip ruminates on more upsides of his wine writing 'job': chairing a literary luncheon for Martin Cruz Smith, 'the whizzbang thriller king' who wrote* Gorky Park *and* Northern Star, *and soon-to-be-published* Red Square. *Then orchestrating poet Les Murray's night at a season of Tapas Readings, organised by The Writers' Centre.*]

The last time I'd seen Les read was years ago, when he arrived just after I'd heard of the death of the great winemaker Stephen Hickinbotham, his lover, Jen, and five other mates from Melbourne. They were in a terrible plane crash near Cairns and Stephen had been my best mate and teacher. I had no chance of coming to grips with a tragedy of this stature – its awful night and mystery had me gasping for breath betwixt sobs. Les had watched and listened for some hours. Then he said: 'I know what happened to your mates. They flew into a cloud with a rock in it.' Instantly, the whole darned mess took on a clear, bright sense. It takes a poet. So here I was last week, introducing a truly great poet. He read in his puffy, soft rush of a way of reading, a little more forceful after five years off the fags, and we surged and subsided with him. Rockford red it was that night and lots of it, swoon.

Kinselas, Sydney, mid-eighties. I'm drinking cognac in the cocktail bar with Adam Wynn: we got a late start: it's 2 am. A short Indian fellow approaches. He's in dark blue drill shirt and pants, like an electrician wears – just like Allen Ginsberg wore continuously through his stay in the early '70s – and he's carrying an airline bag stuffed with newspapers. 'Gentlemen,' he says in a perfect Trinidad-Indian-Oxford-English, 'I admire your attitude to cognac. May I buy you a drink?' We hit it off like a house on fire. The guy's so funny, slapping high fives and hollerin' 'Get down' in faux hillbilly. We drink and laugh, laugh and drink until they gently usher us out into the skinny morning light of Taylor Square. As we bid our farewells I tell Adam, 'I'll see you back at the winery on Wednesday,' referring to his new venture a thousand kays away, on the High Eden Ridge at Mountadam. Our Indian mate suddenly shows a new interest. 'Oh,' he says, 'do you gentlemen have contacts in the wine industry? I plan to visit the South Australian wineries in a few months, when I have finished my work in the Northern Territory.' I mischievously suggest that between Mr Wynn and myself we could arrange the odd good day at a winery sort of thing, and enquire as to the work in the Territory. 'I am writing a book about Australia,' he says, 'about the relationship here between black and white.' Which triggers a raggedly unison 'Well who the hell are you?' He puts forth his hand. 'I am Shiva Naipaul.'

POSTSCRIPT: Shiva, the younger brother of V.S. Naipaul, had written two novels, but I knew him through his prickly acuity in *The Spectator*, and his two riveting travel books, *North of South* and *Black and White*. The former was a wry account of travels in Africa; the latter a terrifying history of the Rev. Jim Jones, and Naipaul's account of visiting the Guyana jungle as officials were still cleaning up bodies after the horror of the Jonestown Massacre. Once his tour of the north of Australia was cut short, Shiva took the spare room for a time in Adelaide while he drank my cellar dry before going back to London to finish his highly contentious and much-publicised book.

But he died suddenly, of a heart attack, at his desk in August '85. His widow, Jenny, later forwarded me an unposted letter she'd found in his papers.

'Life has been hellish', he'd written, 'and somewhat unreal since my return. Hardly had I unpacked my bags when Indira Gandhi was assassinated . . . the next day, at the behest of *The Observer*, I was on my way to Delhi . . . not surprisingly, given the events of the last few weeks, the Antipodes receded from the foreground of my consciousness. I am now faced with the not too easy task of restoring those six months to their proper place. If all goes reasonably well, it should be done by the autumn of '85.' It wasn't of course. Imperfect skerricks of it eventually found their way into *An Unfinished Journey*.

Once one had won his trust, and grown the confidence to ask him, Shiva spoke much of his fear of visiting India. He felt it would flood his writing brain, so nothing else would fit. He'd been born a Brahmin in Trinidad, and admitted that he would never be ready to visit India. It seemed to terrify him. His travail, to look at Indira Gandhi's blood for *The Observer*, must have been deeply confronting.

His was the most challenging, entertaining, vivid intellect I have encountered.

Iceman's Wine Cask Puts the Wowsers on Their Ear

ADVERTISER, 20 JANUARY 1993

The biggest danger inherent in the wowser lobby is its abysmal stupidity. It's selfish, interfering and puritan, holier-than-thou and supremely fascist. Combine all these pathological quirks with self-promoting stupidity and you end up with the ideological equivalent of Idi Amin or Papa Doc – a totally unpredictable loony that makes the cold method of a Hitler seem warm and cosy.

The most recent example of this stupidity centres on Otze the Iceman. This 5300-year-old chap inched from the edge of the Similaun glacier in the Tyrol on 19 September 1991. Since then, he has been the cause of massive international squabbling over his nationality, his age, his reason for being, his nature, and the cause of his death. He has been not only the trigger of endless reams of scientific gobbledegook but also the basis of some absolutely delicious forensic work, and some unseemly public attention. Thousands of women fought to be fertilised by Otze's frozen semen.

The Iceman even made the front cover of *Time* magazine, which informed the aforementioned hopefuls that his scrotum and its contents had been pinched by sightseers before the boffins bothered to extract him from the ice.

But, so far, easily the most entertaining part has been the argument in *Science* magazine. Anthropologists and forensic scientists finally agreed that Otze 'lay down in exhaustion' and 'fell asleep', where he froze to death and was subsequently swallowed by the glacier. Even more specifically, these great scientists reported that Otze had died lying on his side, his head resting on a rock. The reasoning behind all this was a strange fold in the cadaver's left ear.

Since these astonishing revelations, Dr George McManus has written that a folded ear indicates death by the bottle. 'If you're too stewed to straighten your ear out, you've had too much to drink,' Dr McManus claims. He reckons the Tyrolean's last mistake was to guzzle too heartily his prehistoric schnapps.

Horst Seidler, professor at the Vienna Institute of Human Biology, has since replied, partly agreeing, but explaining that his colleagues at the Institute of Alpine History research have so far failed to locate the bottle. Surely, an expert with a wide range of experience as wide as the shipment I have below my belt would immediately reflect upon the hundreds of companions who have left him slumbering harmlessly on his ear. They invariably take the bottle off with them.

Other experts would point out that bottles had not been invented in 2300BC. Some claim the Egyptians did it first in 1500BC. A millennium later, Romans used glass for decanters, but not for takeaways. There are reports from the 13th century of the Mongol Khan accepting shipments of bottle grog from the Muslim countries but it wasn't until the 17th century that bottles were used much. It really began when merchants used them to ship wine from Shiraz, in Persia, to India.

I believe distillation was not yet invented, deftly removing 'prehistoric schnapps' from the equation. The Irish tried for hundreds of years to convince the world they invented distillation. This forced me to plan the securing of a Churchill Fellowship so I could travel to Egypt and prove Coptic missionaries from there took distillation to Ireland in the first few centuries AD. My clever plans were well underway when they were dashed by a brochure from the Irish distillers last year in which they suggested the still probably came to them from Egypt. Damn them.

Otze may have overdone it on wine. And the same freezing that had me first discount this theory now affirms it. But we need a modern example to best explain it. In areas where grapes are over-irrigated and overlooked by too much sun, they yield watery, tasteless juice. Winemakers, somehow, need to give the resultant wine more flavour without breaking the law. So they freeze, say, the bottom 10 per cent of the tank. Water freezes first, leaving a concentrated wine floating on the top. This is racked off, and the frozen water removed.

I believe that if old Otze did go down with a skinful, it was because his skinful had frozen. A thirsty soul, he sucked the few drops of unfrozen juice from it. Magically, that luscious concentrate lifted his soul, filled him with high ambition, and convinced him he could climb higher than ever before. He may even have yodelled. But, later, that same seductive brew told him he could safely lie down in the ice for a bit of a kip. 'Hmmm. That rock'd make a noish pillow. Ahhh. Zzzzzzz.'

Suddenly, 5300 years later, the Similaun glacier changed Otze from jetsam to flotsam, spat him out, and left him for idiot tourists to hack off his privates and pinch his invention: strong cask white.

If the wowser lobby were not so incredibly stupid it would have realised this remarkable yarn is its best chance yet of advertising the demonic evil of the booze. It was killing heroes 5300 years ago. Cheap bag-in-the-box stuff in particular.

NOTE: Decades later, scientists came up with a conclusion that has not been challenged: high in a remote area of the Oetztaler Alps in northern Italy, Otzi was shot in the back with an arrow. It hit a main artery and he probably bled to death within minutes. His body was preserved in the ice, making him one of the oldest and best-preserved mummies on Earth. Heavily tattooed – 61 in all – he was an anatomically modern example of homo sapiens who lived in the Copper Age. No signs of alcohol.

Consto King Takes Hardy Queen

INDEPENDENT WEEKLY, 2 NOVEMBER 2009

I don't know whether McLaren Vale has its own local Bacchus and Pan pulling the strings of its court, but there was some wired poltergeist at work, on somebody's behalf, at the Bushing King crowning on Friday.

One minute I'm up there weeping, taking possession of the revered Trott Family Trophy for my efforts protecting McLaren Vale's dwindling green belt, specifically Glenthorne Farm, and then Paul Carpenter gets up to be crowned king of McLaren Vale's winemakers for a year. Paul's the amiable and respected guy who played a great central role at the Grand Cru show at the Victory a few weeks ago, displaying four reds from different bits of McLaren Vale. On that day, he felt awkward, as he said, representing Constellation at a show for tiny shedsters. The irony lies in the fact that no small Vale Cru-sized winemaker could do what his giant mob could do, and bother to make small batch wines from different sub-regions.

When he got up for his crown in front of the five hundred on Friday, Paul was regal and statesmanly in his clear appreciation and expression that he worked for Constellation. I'd give him a job straight away: he could be in charge of my palace guard. Vigilant loyalty to his employer was the trademark he left there on the air, as the applause took it all away.

But this is the company that has just uprooted John Reynell's famous cabernet and malbec vineyard at Chateau Reynella, where Thomas Hardy got his first vineyard job. So I get a trophy for saving some vineyard land, which still has no vineyard on it, and the bloke who works for the mob who's just ripped out an irreplaceable historical vineyard gets one too. That priceless little block that's disappearing under a ghetto as we speak made good wine for 161 years.

There's more irony in here: nearly a decade ago, when Greg Trott was busy saving Glenthorne, and needed a big winery to agree to take its fruit, it was the pre-Constellation Hardy's that put its huge mitt up in the name of sponsoring essential vineyard research. How times have changed!

Since it has so well and truly trashed so many of its Australian adventures, Constellation has a new morality mantra. Its army of PR flaks have 'defined three areas in which all of its Corporate Social Responsibility focus will take place: sustainable business practices, philanthropy and social responsibility. From these three focus areas flow specific categories of emphasis, including our environmental impact, corporate giving, marketing and advertising codes, community involvement and much more. All of Constellation's social responsibility efforts flow directly from its values and culture'.

But there was another delicious layer of irony, as thick as whipped cream. The new King Paul was accompanied by one of the enormous Hardy tribe, a descendant of Thomas Hardy. This was Alix Hardy, whom Paul has chosen to be his queen for a year.

Now this was Friday, remember. My paper, Adelaide's brave little *Independent Weekly*, that morning ran my piece examining

Constellation's new corporate mantra and strange panicky behaviour. This (see below) went round the world rather quickly, with links appearing on boozy hives like Dr. Vino. For some reason, on Sunday, Constellation felt obliged to make a statement. This contained little that was new. Basically it's the collision of two great husks: one, the shell of Constellation Australia, rattling emptily with the remains of all the great companies and properties that leviathan has gutsed up, trying to make some sort of sicko procreative act with the great husk of Australian Vintage Limited. This latter lot, the remnants of Brian McGuigan's third empire, had even taken his name off its flag to make things look better. To no avail. McGuigan, Simeon, Australian Vintage, Galaxy, Milky Way, Universal – doesn't matter what it's called. It has always spent a lot of its time in the shallow edges of wine's gene pool.

Which is not to say these great corporations can't make good wine, of course: Australian Vintage's Nepenthe gets regular gongs, and Constellation, as well as the Bushing Trophy, has absolutely cleaned up at the Royal (yep, they still call them that), at the Royal wine shows of Adelaide and Perth.

So on Sunday, Constellation Brands Inc., the world's largest winemaker, releases a statement from its CEO, Rob Sands, which says: 'The Australian wine industry is facing unprecedented negative operating conditions.' And suggested that if a deal could be done with Australian Vintage, where Constellation swapped some of its carcases for a substantial equity stake, but not a controlling one, the new combo 'would create synergies between the two companies, better positioning the new entity for success in the current challenging operating environment'.

If a transaction results, the combined companies would operate as a stand alone wine company, which would be listed on the Australian Stock Exchange, but typically, Sands also said the talks with Australian Vintage are preliminary and may not lead to a transaction. The company didn't identify any other potential partners. But there was one pretty obvious one on the stage at the Bushing lunch, being crowned queen of Constellation's new king.

There has been a quiet, somewhat ungainly attempt at courtship with certain branches of the Hardy family tree, with Constellation exploring the possibility of the lovely Hardys finding the money to take Chateau Reynella back off its hands.

Which would go some way to explaining why key Hardy wine men who were first aghast at the notion of Constellation uprooting the first vineyard their great founder worked in, suddenly withdrew their support from my failed campaign to save Reynell's priceless little vine garden.

And why not one squeak of support from the stupidly named McLaren Vale Grape Wine And Tourism Association in my battle for the Reynella vineyard? Like why did I lose? Partly because everyone who may have been likely to voice some enragement depend upon Constellation buying their grapes. And partly because, whatever its name at the time, that association has been fed for decades by funds from the Hardy Family, from Hardy's Reynella, from BRL-Hardy, and then Constellation. Now that money's drying up, maybe even the McLVGWATA's sufficiently swift to sniff the disappearing possibility of the odd pound note wafting down from the tables of whichever Hardys would be crazy and/or brave enough to have another go at what has already proved to be beyond them.

Those Hardys meanwhile, whom are serious grape-growers, must feel rather uncomfortable about just who will be buying their grapes should the remnants of their old family show finally die in bed with Australian Vintage.

Not to go on too much about the work of Constellation's

incredible PR hacks, but the last bit of their Sunday statement more or less said it all.

'This news release contains forward-looking statements', it said. 'The words 'anticipate', 'intend', and 'expect', and similar expressions are intended to identify forward-looking statements, although not all forward-looking statements contain such identifying words. These statements may relate to Constellation's business strategy, future operations, prospects, plans and objectives of management, as well as information concerning expected actions of third parties. All forward-looking statements involve risks and uncertainties that could cause actual results to differ materially from those set forth in or implied by the forward-looking statements.'

Pulling No Punches, Biting the Hand that Bleeds

INDEPENDENT WEEKLY, 30 DECEMBER 2009

'Do you know anything about finance?' Jim Ingoldby glowered.

'No,' I said.

'Good,' he said. 'Now we can talk.'

I'd known Jim for twenty-five years. But this was a different day: I was suddenly there in his home as his fair daughter Jane's partner. His wry opener was an indicator of his intention to hang on to the family coffers as much as his disbelief at what was happening to the wine industry.

Jim died of long life a few months back, one of the last of the great postwar winemakers. He had stacked many a gift beneath the Christmas trees, allegorical or real, of his friends, family and employees through his amazingly creative life, and as

I contemplate whether indeed to bother with a bauble fir on the occasion of Jesus' 2009th birthday, I know Jim would ridicule my sentiment, but love playing with the wires and lights.

I'd recall asking Ian Sutton, Chief Executive of the Winemakers' Federation of Australia, Wine Australia Pty Ltd, Australian Wine Foundation and the Australian Wine and Brandy Producers' Association, which bits of the wine industry he'd consulted about his determined putsch to use $40 or 50 million of the taxpayers' money to build the National Wine Centre in the Botanic Gardens. Sutton snarled, 'My job's not to consult the wine industry – my job is to represent the wine industry.' Great.

That ugly pile in the Gardens is the perfect allegory for the way the whole business has gone crook. Those who put it there should be drawn to account, if not drawn and quartered. They should never be let near the levers of wine industry power, ever again. But still they hover. 'This taxpayer-funded Xanadu will have little purpose beyond housing the bureaucrats who will be responsible for the next taxpayer-funded Vine-pull Scheme', I wrote at the time. Touché?

I would recall with Jim his early days at McLaren Flat, where at Rycroft, in the seventies, he radically marketed McLaren Vale wines in bottles labelled according to the vineyards and growers whose wine glowered within – something that is finally, sensibly becoming vogue. I would recall his early adoption of the screw cap, and the ingenious machine he built to apply them. I would revel in his exquisite watercolours: always a new'un on the easel at the end of his bed. And we would roar with derisive laughter and rage at the squirming idiots who, until just a year and a half ago, were urging growers to plant more chardonnay, lay more irrigation pipes, and guarantee an endless supply of fruit at prices so low whole communities would inevitably collapse, along with the river that nurtured them.

If you could squeeze another gift beneath my tree, it should be one more bottle of shiraz with the amazing Jean Paxton, who also left us this year, at the grand old knock of 102. Jean, Mum of David, had watched their family business march bravely out of almond growing and into viticulture. She saw her son move from an aggressive developer of inspired, but industrial, vineyards to become one of the first converts to biodynamic principles and sustainable natural practices, and eventually marry Ang, formally entwining 'Them Paxtons' with the vinous blood of the great Tolley and Penfold families. When she was a hundred, Jean proposed marriage to me: the only lass to ever do so. She mischievously joked that David would be annoyed at me 'getting all the money', and reassured me 'but don't worry – you wouldn't have to put up with me for long'.

At 101 years, this mighty woman triggered a frisson of panic when she was found face down on the floor of her unit, looking for all the world like she'd had a big stroke. There were ambulances, and drips and whatnot, and the usual jittery concerns. But when her family arrived at casualty, a good nurse relieved their fears. It wasn't so bad. They'd just checked her blood alcohol: 0.13. Jean had been enjoying a bottle or two of the sublime Paxton Jean Shiraz, the pinnacle of her son's endeavour, which had been named after her. She couldn't understand the fuss.

I could go on with my festive cheer. But about forty per cent of the wine business won't. It's finished.

A History of Drinking

INDAILY, OPINION, 13 AUGUST 2013

How did the tradition of sitting together at a table and drinking wine begin? Philip White *writes on the history of plonk the way he hopes it will be remembered, and blames it all on the elephants.*

I've been having a recurring dream. I'm sitting in the pastis bar on the edge of the Rhône at Tournon, drinking the Ricard 51. Which number is an indicator of its alcohol. My companion is Lord Twining, noticeable for his full beard. He drinks the candle and sets fire to his face. Can't quite place it, but I have a nagging suspicion this happened, if somewhere else. Might have been in the Botanic in the noughties, when the ancient peer's girlfriend often sat under the table. I don't think it was sado-mas. She just seemed to feel safer down there when the table was awash. She was a tiny dancer. It woulda been safer.

It started under the marula tree. My photographer mate Milton Wordley suggested I write about why we sit around tables, drinking wine with each other. I always thought it would have been a very early mob of us watching the elephants get drunk after eating too much over-ripe marula fruit then drinking water so this king-hell ferment takes off in their giant gizzards and when we were gibbons or whatever we were we copied them and invented wine.

Because it looked like fun.

I was heartbroken to discover that the purist bastards at *National Geographic* calculated that it would take nearly two litres of pure ethanol to get a proper pachyderm tipsy, in which case it would take 27 litres of marula juice at seven per cent alcohol to come up with that much goonbag. They reckon an elephant would therefore have to guts at least 1400 rotten boozy fruits to get shickered, which they think was below the style of your average tasteful elephant, who would of course prefer the fresher fruit. I still reckon a good elephant could get a liking for the boozy fruit.

Somebody invented it. Humans couldna invented it. Humans copy stuff.

A camel can drink 120 litres of water in 10 minutes, so I sort of trust the girth of the elephant to offer a much bigger tank, and if that was already fizzing with marula fruit on the turn . . .

I'm resistant to the suggestion that the recipe was written by a drinker. Given the lack of laptops and the way experimental drinkers work, I don't believe an early convert to ethanol would have recorded the recipe. They were all far too busy developing the market. The recipe would have been written down by one of the forerunners of the *National Geographic*: some horn-rimmed dude with a jacket full of pockets and pens and a keen sense of observation. A friggin wine writer! An early blogger would have got it published on the tom-toms of the day and it would have spread. Five minutes later, everybody's sitting round listening to the boom-boom glossies and they're into gastroporn and drinking wine.

But now, it just can't be accepted that an elephant could get properly plonked. Something obviously went wrong at the *National Geographic*. If elephants never got plonked, who the hell did we copy? The really tricky bit of the history of booze is the emergence of the alembic. The still. When it became apparent that the primitive still could concentrate the colour black for al kohl, the concentrate of lead sulphide worn as eyeliner in north Africa, some clever nutter worked out that it could also be used for concentrating the fragrant essences of plants and their flowers to make perfume, which led to the next genius trying it on beer, or wine, to make what my Shetland grandmother daintily called *spurruts*.

Looks like the Irish pinched distillation from the Moors, while the Vikings found it in the Mediterranean and took it back up the rivers to Russia to invent vodka. Vodka, the water that does not freeze on that long cold row from Scandinavia to Iceland or further, like to the prime real estate developments of Greenland last time things warmed up.

Or on that dragon boat of lads that set out from Bergen, Norway, to row to Shetland, missed it their vodka haze, and discovered America halfway through their hangover. Vinland, see. Rootstocks for 800 years later, when phylloxera ate Europe and the only way you could get vines to grow was to graft them onto American rootstocks. So you could sit around the table together and drink.

If you had a barrel of water on the longboat, it would freeze, and there's not much firewood in the North Atlantic Ocean to make a blaze – on the floor of your wooden boat – to melt it. If your vodka started to freeze, on the other hand, that indicated a fellow rower had taken more than a fair share and topped it up with rain.

Sharpen up the axes.

This is not what you'd call your actual history, but I long ago taught myself that history is gossip written by the winner, while gossip is history related by the loser. Both these theses are applicable here. The ethanol business, that vast tentacular money-making beast which writes all the history because that's what it actually did, actually does write the history.

Gossip? Since the great newspapers carked and spat all their wine writers against the internet, where many of them will not stick, the wine bloggers run the gossip. This is of course unacceptable and totally out of control.

But your actual spread of folks sitting round a table drinking starts in ancient China and Phoenecia and the old Greece and Caucasian Georgia, and if Mr Miles the Poetry Editor forgives me for crossing his patch, I'd like to give you a good old Viking poem, written by the Icelander bard Snorri Sturluson nearly a thousand years ago.

Röst gefr ödlingr iastar
– öl virdi esvá – fyrdum.
Thögn fellir brim bragna
– biórr forn er that – horna.
Máls kann mildingr heilsu
– miödr heitir svá – veita.
Strúgs kemr í val veiga
– vín kallak that – galli.

Which means that while the boss Viking gives floods of fresh yeasty ale to the troops they prefer the older lagered beer in their horns. To get them back on the conversational track, the King pours mead. But to really have the whole saga sung, he pours wine, and guarantees dignity's destruction.

Which is bad news for blokes like John Rau, the attorney-general who tries hard to sort out our vicious drinking laws by weaning us off the *spurruts* and onto the more genteel vinous bevvies. Add this hard intelligence to what he's learnt from the Georgians, the Phoenecians, the Greeks and the good folks round at Pernod-Ricard, who just happen to own Jacob's Creek, and we sort of wobble straight back into Milton's initial query about why we sit down together at tables and drink.

Blame it on the elephants, I say. If you need any clarity, first extinguish the candle, then ask Lord Twining.

Blue Pyrenees Shiraz 2012

$24; 14.5% alcohol; screw cap; 89+ points

INDAILY, 9 OCTOBER 2014

They were grand old days when the wicked Francois Henri was redesigning the Blue Pyrenees vineyard his employer, Remy Martin, had originally planted in the 60s to make premium brandy. The brandy business was taxed into oblivion in the early 70s. Out came the brandy grapes in the ensuing decade; in went the standard red varieties of the day. Colin Lanceley was called in to paint the vineyard beneath the full moon and Francois had a handsome label designed which copied the packaging of Rothmans International cigarettes, a deluxe brand of extra-long smokes for duty-free airport stores. That label was ultra-radical in its day, not because it was influenced by the tobacco business, but because it was blue, a definite no-no for wine in those days. We were tasting the components for his red blend, which was a Bordeaux-style mix with a little Shiraz, when I convinced him the peppery, feisty, young-vine Shiraz was so good it should have its own label.

A game and adventurous soul, Francois called it Australis, as he hoped it would be exported to France, to show the Rhone blokes a thing or two. Here, it was considered one of the better early cool-climate shiraz offerings of its day. Remy hit the international financial shell grit eventually, and retired hurt. After one thing and another, a group of investors bought the business in 2002.

Keeping in mind my sentimental connection, permit me to suggest this is a warmer, softer red than its zappy ancestor. Now those vines are hitting some proper age, it's rich without being strong, and more mellow and soulful. It's not at all gloopy or jammy. It has a dark damp earth and tomato bush aroma, in with its old leather upholstery and polished walnut wood: it smells like an old Jaguar with a warm engine, an oil leak and potted tomato plants on the back seat. Maybe some mushrooms, too. It calmly settles in on the mouth without any challenge. Settle into it, and it's a nostalgic sort of a ride. The tannins are fine and dry and drawn out, and seem well suited to tea-smoked duck or roast quail with pine nuts, reduced spinach on the side. It's no grand cru, but a good drink for the money and, stylistically, a bit of a rarity.

The Trouble with Abstinence

INDAILY, OPINION, 3 FEBRUARY 2015

Coming from an ancestry loaded with insatiable boozers and sanctimonious evangelical teetotallers – not many in between – this writer finds stuff like Febfast and Dry July about as useful as a knock on the door from the Jehovah's Witnesses.

When Sam Clemens – aka Mark Twain – was asked by a reporter at a Melbourne press conference where he'd be going after his death, he shot back 'Heaven for the lifestyle; Hell for the company', which as far as I know was the first recorded usage of the term lifestyle. As this Febfast orgy of denial seems to me to be a lifestyle issue, it's worth wondering about whether having died with a perfect liver you'd prefer to spend eternity singing hymns upstairs around God's big organ with millions of Lutherans, or sit downstairs by the fire with folks like me.

In other words, with all respect due Mr Twain, bugger the lifestyle Heaven has to offer. And the company. There'll be plenty of Febfasters and Dry Julyars up there. The only reason I can think of visiting the Heavenly throng would be to check whether Beethoven's playing the organ with God turning the pages, or vice-versa.

As far as I know, my father's only slip occurred when he and his father visited the white Russian refugee family over the road. I have a very vague memory of sneaking out with the women of the household to watch the two of them crawling home through the pines after a night on the homemade vodka. It was about the same time as we went out to watch the Sputnik go over, and seemed to be on par with that as far as important events went. Dad devoted the rest of his life in the redemption business. Apart from his regular pastoral duties, he spent years in some vague sort of management position at the Women's Christian Temperance Union, which never seemed to have any women on the board.

As a teenager, my mum got drunk and chundered on a ride at Luna Park when she ran away from home. She never boozed again. When I was about 40 I tried to explain to her what Château d'Yquem tasted like, and she said, 'Ewwww, Philip, you know I'd love it that much I'd be an instant alcoholic,' and that was about as far as that ever went.

My brothers and I were all trained to tip out wine and beer if we could find any, like in the back of cars of drunks and vagabonds when they called in to the Old Man's parsonage for a free feed. Sometimes I run into blokes I can't quite recall, and they immediately remind me that I owe them a dozen long necks of Coopers or whatever.

In her recent BBC piece, 'Australia's new non-drinking puritans', Madeleine Morris reports meeting the sort of person I once was. Chris Raine, 'an affable 26-year-old', runs a thing called Hello Sunday Morning, a 'charity that encourages people to take a break from booze for between three and 12 months, and blog about it'. 'You'd think that if you go into a bar and tell people your job is to tell people not to drink for three months then they would scatter, but people are really interested,' he told her 'over a chocolate milkshake in a trendy Melbourne café'. Over a chocolate milkshake, see? Late weaner? As for a blog written about not drinking? Thank God I was healed of my proho wowserism at the age of 18, grew up, and spent my whole life since kicking for the boho team.

There's a wave of dry interferist nonsense flooding the media as I write: reams of pseudo-medical stuff about self-deception and self-worth and lurid descriptions of what a certain number of drinks per week can do to your pancreas or liver.

My dad's brother, Robert, drank metho for about 30 years after his oilrig money ran out. He could drink quite a lot of it, neat, and laughed all the time. Twice he underwent surgery to have great lumps of liver chopped out but when he died after a two-bottle binge in his late 60s, the post mortem said there was no liver left. He lasted a lot longer than the shadow-boxing Terry O'Rielly, another infamous drunk whose brother was the Governor of Northern Ireland. Terry lived in Victoria Square in a suit and tie, reciting endless reams of James Joyce and Sam Beckett. His fallback tincture was unique: he'd put a slice of toast on an empty soup tin, tip a can of Brasso through it, and sink the strained spurruts in a gulp.

These are the sorts of consumption which need mental health attention before the liver cleaver comes into action, or the sanctimonious start hovering around, preaching. Unfortunately, mental health seems to have vanished as an issue if Australian budget allocations are any measure.

The daily dependence such alcoholics suffer is rarely solved by

Febfasts or Dry Julys. Not to pick on the Lutherans, I was always fascinated by the Barossa's respect of Lent. For the whole six weeks from Ash Wednesday to Easter Sunday they won't touch a drop. Then they have the decidedly moist Vintage Festival, where dancing on the tables is verboten, but Lent seems quickly outdone by the feasting and dancing on tables which that beautifully organised riot incurs.

To reinforce my belief that there are a lot more old drunks than old doctors, one moderate theory comes from nutritionist Professor Charles Bamforth of the University of California, Davis. Of course he agrees that drinking too much is plain silly, just like eating too much. But just as there's a difference between eating too much salad and stuffing yourself to bursting point eating Maccas, the Prof insists that care in the choice of drink is as important as the volume. Like there'd be a health difference between Red Bull with Baileys and a butcher of real ale, or a glass of organic red wine.

'The key is a little and often,' he says. 'You are seriously mistaken if you think that having a month without drinking will protect you from the effects of excessive drinking for the rest of the year . . . The best advice is to drink moderately throughout the year . . . Many people don't realise that drinking in moderation has significant health benefits and that moderate drinkers have a longer life expectancy than non-drinkers . . . Regular moderate intake of alcohol is good for the heart and blood circulation.

'The great thing about beer,' he continues, 'is that it is low in alcohol and brewed from natural raw materials so it's a good source of important nutrients such as antioxidants, B vitamins and dietary silicon that promotes strong bones . . . Indeed beer used to be known as liquid bread.'

My preferred degree of abstinence was that maintained by Sir Frank Renouf, the Kiwi tycoon who was for a time married to

Susan Peacock/Sangster/Renouf. Sir Frank was a good bloke, and when I spent a few days with them in the late 80s he was a hale and hearty gentleman in his 70s who carried his tennis racket everywhere. As I learned when taking him to visit Marg and Peter Lehmann and Wyndham and Helen Hill Smith during a stay in Adelaide, he was also a thirsty old rogue.

When I asked the secret of his radiant fitness, his response was so simple as to stun. 'I drink only on alternate days,' he said. 'Every second day I abstain.' The old rascal went on to explain that the habitual boozer is often corralled by regular events, like after work on Friday nights, when one tends to make a bit of a mess. By rigidly holding to his schedule, such routines are soon broken.

Sir Frank went on to live another decade. I'll bet he's not singing hymns with the Lutherans.

The Stoner's Wine Companion

INDAILY, WINE, 23 OCTOBER 2018

Liquor is quicker? Pot is not? Philip White *says it's time we forgot the puerile '50s wit of Ogden Nash and prepared for a new world of intoxicating literature.*

For a Scandinavian wine blog, David Morrison's *The Wine Gourd* spends quite a lot of its time examining Australian wine and the way Oz critics score wine.

Yesterday the *Gourd* reminded us of two recent articles which examine the erratic nature of wine scores, not just across different tasters but also the variations within a single critic's scores of the same wine tasted on different occasions. These are analysed from a number-cruncher's point of view: the cold hard statistics, on the record, surely deserve some examination.

Of course the human reaction to something as fleeting and moody as wine varies. It alters from room-to-room, lab-to-lab, day-to-day and season-to-season, and, given the vagaries of cork, from bottle-to-bottle. Ambient aromas, colour and noise – like music or conversation – can radically alter the way we interpret wines to ourselves, even before we attempt the risky trick of trying to explain our reaction to others – in a language poorly equipped with words specific to aroma and flavour. This is partly why we resort to point or star scores: since we learned to count with some proficiency, many humans seem more likely to respect a simple numerical evaluation than they tend to believe or attempt to understand a written or recited review.

For which they can't be blamed, given the literary capacities of many wine 'experts'. This writer's mantra has generally spun around the suspicion that wine scores are used by critics with little faith in their own writing and descriptive skills when they attempt to influence the buying patterns of people whose reading capacities and comprehension they similarly mistrust. Such inadequate simplistic rankings, of course, are used with withering efficiency by discounting retailers, especially if they can influence the results of grand mega-tastings with their advertising dollar and corner the market of the winning wines. Which they do.

Similarly, wine show results are always influenced by the judges selected for the job. Tell me the style of wine you want rewarded with major bling at your next regional wine races and I'll pick you a team of judges to deliver precisely that result. At least we seem now to have a choice: do we take our wine-buying advice from the math teacher, the English teacher, or the gastronome? The faceless white coat or the vagabond who's off their face? The poet or the statistician? A bit of a dab of each seems a surefire system.

Typically, in the same inbox as the *Gourd's* missive came another, more challenging yarn from the cannabis connoisseur's website, *Leafly*. It's a classic toe in the water of a new genre of epicurean literature: *How to Pair Food and Drinks With Cannabis Terpenes.*

Oh lordy. If the *Gourd* finds irritating the lack of consistency humans show when ranking grape-based ethanol drinks, without even beginning to scratch their increasing vagary with the introduction of accompanying foods, Bacchus knows we're going to see some funny stuff emerge with the introduction of another powerful psychoactive ingredient.

As one country or province after another lifts the century-old prohibitions on the myriad forms of cannabis available, and the stock exchangers and Coke plunge in with their billions, the amount of money being spent on publications, scientific research, sophisticated processing tools for the kitchen and whatnot is phenomenal. It's a bit like all the paraphernalia and *accoutrements* required for the refined preparation and consumption of alcohol, tobacco, coffee, tea, chocolate, half of gastronomy and the entire pharmacopoeia is suddenly required, for the first time, all at once.

Consider: The American Academy of Cannabinoid Medicine alone lists more than 25,000 articles on cannabis, cannabinoids and the endocannabinoid system published in peer-reviewed medical journals since 1995. It's on.

The drinks fascinate this drinks critic: huge trans and multinational liquor and beverage manufacturers, from wineries through brewers to lolly-water/kiddylikker suppliers, are into cannabis drinks big time. The first had little or no alcohol and not much of your actual stone, but quickly we see these ingredients playing a larger role, sometimes in the same vessel.

Remember when pot was always *verboten*? Then, as it gradually became more acceptable, if still illicit, the one rule never to be broken: 'Don't mix pot and liquor'? Like the shibboleth about combining caffeine and ethanol, those days are very quickly receding into the past. They will soon be over. People have learned to have a cognac and a coffee without carking it. Folks are learning very quickly to manage their own dosage. With better, more fact-based education, this will increase.

Just like we were taught for years to avoid taking paracetamol with ibuprofen, we are now discovering a little of each is more beneficial in many cases, sometimes even giving the opiates a run for their money in the efficacy stakes. So, in an unholy melding of the inevitabilities, let's wonder how *The Wine Gourd* and its like will handle the biggest new variable: how will the presence of pot influence the way in which the Jeremy Olivers, Jeni Ports and James Hallidays review, rank and describe cannabis-infused wine? Not only does cannabis influence aroma and flavour, immediately calling for a whole new vocabulary, but its incredible range of psychoactive effects will also deserve explanation. Our critics are going to have to learn to describe relative intoxications.

The earliest Australian wine reporters, like Ebenezer Ward (1837–1917) and Ernest Whitington (1873–1934) reported mainly numbers and details: gastronomic evaluation was rarely, if ever, attempted. After World War II, writers like Walter James and Osmar White began to cross over toward ranks and scores, but never quite got there. Dear Walter, for example, liked referring to how well his wines 'went with chops'.

It was the Len Evanses, the Ian Hickinbothams and James Hallidays, the Di Holuigues and Geraldine Pascales that tipped in the indulgence, in the 70s recognising the synergies that arise when ethanol is included in epicurean literature. And I mean included, not just in its material combinations like the actual food and wine, but in its interpretation, and the manner of its printed presentation, the mood of the writing as much as vocabulary, syntax and grammar.

Gone are the days when the business would wince and flinch when the likes of Evans wrote something like: 'Port makes you fart.' The next James Halliday will need to be an erudite stoner.

Index

Wakefield Press

Blood on the Typewriter

Robbie Brechin is a journalist of four decades' experience, working across print, radio and television, covering fields from politics to rock music and nightlife. He lives in Adelaide.

Light and dark. Philip, X-rayed by his friend, cartoonist George Grainger Aldridge.